SOMEWHERE COLD

A memoir

SOMEWHERE COLD

A memoir

GERALDINE OSBORNE

Bergs near Grise Fiord. Oil on canvas. Danny Osborne

MERCIER PRESS

For Sufyaan, Maya Rosa, Abdullah, Greta, Aminah and Aven.

MERCIER PRESS
Cork
www.mercierpress.ie

© Geraldine Osborne, 2025
© Illustrations – Danny Osborne
© Photos – Geraldine & Danny Osborne

ISBN: 978-1-78117-877-5

Cover design: Craig Carry

This book is sold subject to the condition that it shall not, by way of trade or otherwise, be lent, resold, hired out or otherwise circulated without the publisher's prior consent in any form of binding or cover other than that in which it is published and without a similar condition including this condition being imposed on the subsequent purchaser.

No part of this publication may be reproduced or transmitted in any form or by any means, electronic or mechanical, including photocopying, recording or any information or retrieval system, without the prior permission of the publisher in writing.

Printed in the EU.

And I think over again
My small adventures
When with a shore wind I drifted out
In my kayak
And thought I was in danger.
My fears,
Those small ones
That I thought so big,
For all the vital things
I had to get and to reach.

And yet, there is only
One great thing,
The only thing:
To live to see in huts and on journeys
The great day that dawns,
And the light that fills the world.

Translation of Inuit poem, Carpenter, E., 'Eskimo Realities', by permission from the Rock Foundation/Estate of Edmund Carpenter

Arctic Regions

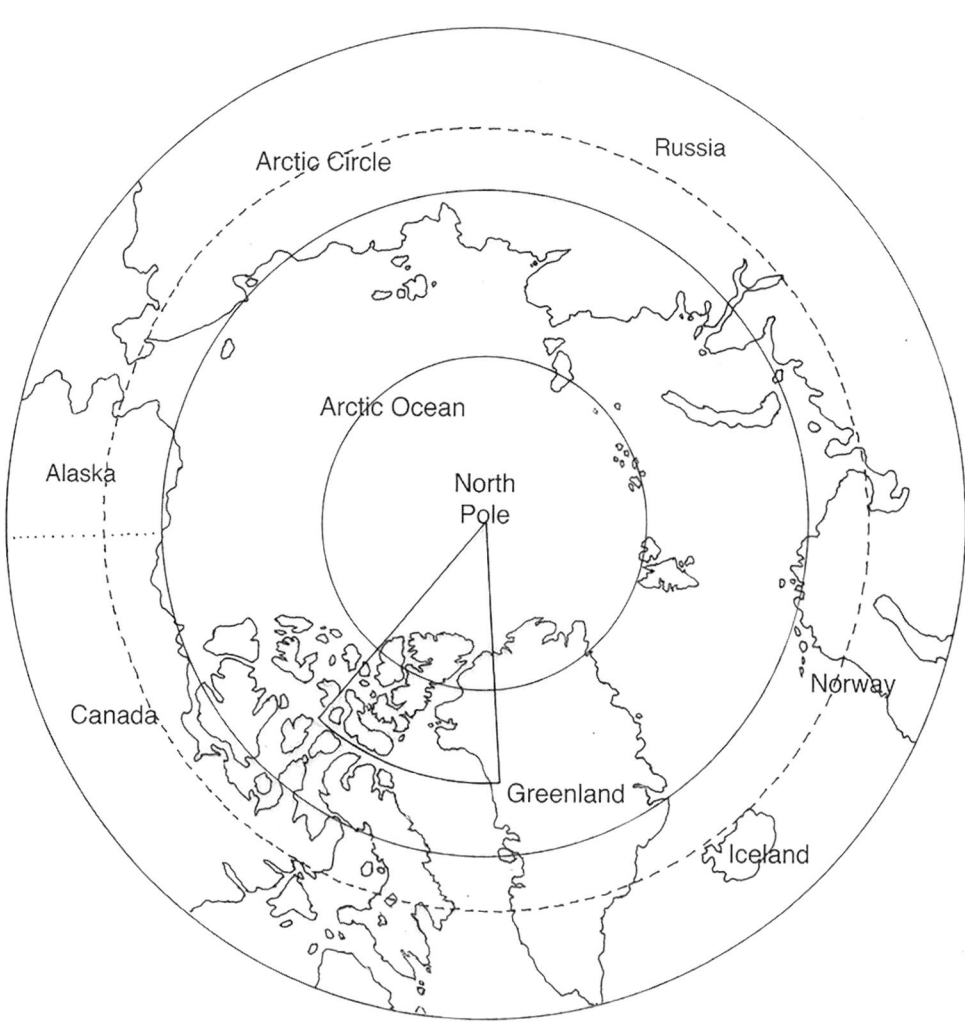

Acknowledgements

A huge thank you to all the people of Grise Fiord, especially the Akeeagok family, the Kiguktak family, the Audlaluk family, the Pijamini family, and the Flahertys, whose kindness, generosity and good humour made Grise Fiord a very warm place to live in. Also, the people of Qaanaaq, especially our friends, Naduk and Suulut Rasmussen, who helped us in any way they could. It was a privilege to spend time living with them in that wonderful part of the world. Thanks too to the Hamlet of Grise Fiord and the Mayor of Qaanaaq for welcoming us, and to Brent Boddy, Bryan Pearson and Ken McRury for their advice and hospitality in Iqaluit.

Many thanks to Tempy Osborne and Maeve O'Neill for helping with the photographs, to Beth Tyrrell and Tempy Cummins for being so encouraging in the early days of writing this book, to Mary Feehan, Dee Collins and Carina McNally of Mercier Press for their support, and to Danny for sharing his journals and sketch book drawings as well as his love and enthusiasm for the Arctic.

Chapter One

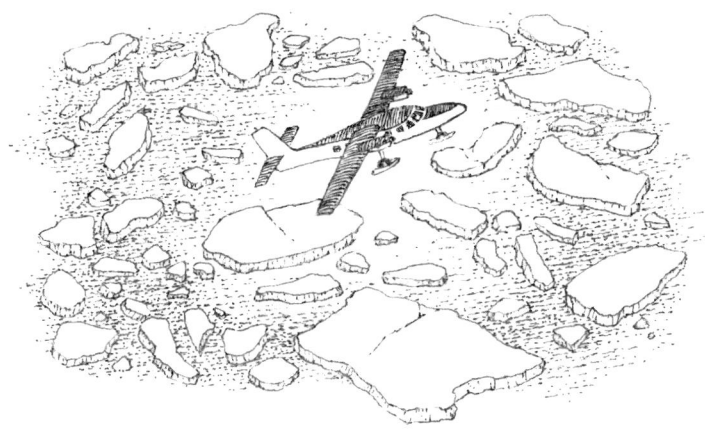

Crammed into a small Twin Otter aeroplane, behind boxes of fruit, bread and other supplies for the local shop, my young family and our nine cowering sled dogs were about to land in one of the coldest, most remote communities on earth. Strapped into her seat, two-year-old Orla slept while baby Oisín, on my knee, constantly pulled his socks off, baiting a fierce-looking black dog with his plump toes. Due to a lack of space on the aeroplane, the dogs, new recruits to the family, were tied behind and under our seats because their regulation crates had been ditched at our previous stop, the small airport at Resolute Bay. Normally, such proximity to each other would cause ferocious fighting, but shaken by their terror of flying, they could only muster the occasional snarl.

'I can't put my feet down'. Our five-year-old, Tempy, pouted, pointing to Minnie Mouse, a small husky sleeping under her seat.

'I know, I have a dog under my seat too, so does Orla, but look – I can see the sea.' I peered through the tiny ice-coated window. 'We're almost there!'

The thick, gloomy fog obscuring our view flying over Cornwallis Island, Wellington Channel and Devon Island dissipated, revealing a jigsaw of ice floes cluttering a blue-black sea.

'That's Jones Sound, won't be long now.' Danny shouted over the engine's din, hemmed in by our crates of gear stacked at the plane's rear.

Staring at the ice-studded Arctic waters with excitement and a nip of trepidation, my mind raced, coming to terms with the new reality ahead of us. Only two weeks ago, at the end of summer 1989, we had locked up our cottage on the south-western tip of Ireland and began our journey north to spend a year living in Grise Fiord, a tiny Inuit hamlet on Ellesmere Island, over 1,000 kilometres above the Arctic Circle. The thought that we were crossing paths with the Brent Geese I had often seen along Dublin Bay in my student days struck me. They were leaving Ellesmere, flying to the Irish coastline to escape the long, freezing winter ahead, as we abandoned such prudence and flew in the opposite direction.

Although I'd travelled a lot, the furthest north I'd ever ventured was to Scotland, but Danny was no stranger to Arctic life. As an artist, he had spent three months in the Inuit community of Qiqiktarjuaq on Baffin Island in 1977, where he painted icescapes in oils and watercolours and was captivated by the austere beauty of the place. He was equally attracted to the adventure of exploration. During his second trip in 1981, as one of three members of the First Irish Arctic Expedition, he travelled solo for weeks in the uninhabited north-west interior of Ellesmere Island. Danny's love of all things polar, as well as his unflagging optimism, was contagious. To be out on the sea ice, far away from any signs of civilisation, painting untouched vistas that have changed little over millennia, was for him sublime, and for me, the lure of the unknown outweighed any forebodings of danger, isolation, and loneliness.

Growing up, my parents rarely went anywhere, apart from summers spent with relatives in the countryside of North Tipperary, which felt like paradise for a small child from a housing estate in a midland town.

But from a young age, I was aware that we are part of a mysterious, wider world where people live entirely different lives from my narrow existence, gleaned mainly from reading and television. This opened my eyes, and I couldn't wait to go further afield as soon as possible. At the age of sixteen, my school friend Monica and I found summer jobs at a hotel in Kerry, and as my mother later told me, from then on, 'I was gone'. During my final years at school, I worked hard to get a place in Medicine at university. My somewhat naive ambition was to practise as a doctor in some far-off, underdeveloped region of the world. As I cycled to school, I daydreamed I was on ships bound for foreign lands, where I could immerse myself in a new culture and meet different people while providing medical assistance. That plan got side-tracked after I married Danny. Although we did travel to far-flung places, we could never bring the children. But this time, the whole family could travel together to live in Grise Fiord, the only Inuit hamlet on Ellesmere Island, and undertake a long journey by dog team across the frozen sea to Greenland. Beyond Grise Fiord, the atlas showed mountains covered in ice caps, glaciers and the Arctic Ocean with the elusive North Pole. It seemed the most exotic venture possible.

Finding specific information on this tiny Inuit community before the availability of the internet or the World Wide Web was difficult. Still, through some of Danny's Canadian friends, I learned that the population was less than 100, Inuktitut was the spoken language. Although most people were employed, hunting was still the main preoccupation. In an article about Grise Fiord in *National Geographic*, I spotted a photo of carefree kids playing outside their school in the snow. Danny assured me that the Inuit are the most child-centred people he had ever encountered, the ideal place to bring our kids. Living at a latitude of over seventy-six degrees north meant the sun would not appear over the horizon for three months of winter, while the thermometer would stay below at least -30° Celsius. I couldn't imagine a more alien environment to live on earth – perfect for experiencing a totally different life.

Barren brown hills powdered with snow appeared on the horizon as the plane began its descent, and minutes later, a line of tiny houses edging the shoreline came into view. Then we lost altitude and alarmingly headed straight on a collision course for those steep hills. Bracing myself, I hugged Oisin tightly, as the plane banked sharply to the left, the wing tip almost touching the cliff above. These aerial manoeuvres triggered deafening howls from all the dogs, waking Orla. Both sisters, stunned by the noise and chaos stared in silence at Rambo attacking and ripping apart a box of bread beside him, followed by a frenzied tearing at the seat to which he was tethered.

'Don't worry, we'll be getting out now', I said as the plane eased down to a gravel riverbed, shaking in the crosswinds coming off the ice cap above. Balloon tyres touched the ground while the engines reached an ear-splitting crescendo, drowning the clamour of the dogs, before coming to an abrupt halt. Calm then descended as the plane purred and snowflakes floated to earth outside.

'Wow, that was dramatic.' I gasped, turning towards Danny.

'I thought we weren't going to make it at one stage,' he laughed, getting out of his seat and making for the door. 'It's probably just another routine touchdown for the people here. We'll get the children out first, then take the dogs.'

Relief at arriving was short-lived. The pilot opened the door, filling the plane with a blast of icy Arctic air and the dogs lurched towards him. Keen to unload his cargo and get out of this godforsaken place, he began to untie them.

'You'll get a bill for this,' he mumbled when he saw the Rambo-damaged seat.

Passing the children over to Danny, I noticed a small gathering of people outside and hoped they would help us disembark, but they all drew back at the sight of our dogs. Mike, a government representative and Fred, the Royal Canadian Mounted Police (RCMP) officer, came forward to introduce themselves and help us unload. Terry, Mike's partner and resident nurse, was waiting to board the plane to fly to Iqaluit for a nursing conference. She introduced me to Ooleesie, a small grey-haired woman standing beside her. Like most elders here, she spoke Inuktitut with a few words of English.

'Leave the children and come and help get the dogs off the plane,' Danny shouted to me, grabbing two dogs by their leads.

'I can't, I have Oisín.' With Oisín in my arms, I thought I would be spared handling the dogs until I got to know them better.

'Just leave him there, on the ground,' he pointed to the frozen gravel, 'it won't take long. We can't have these dogs loose here.'

I scanned the rugged terrain for a safe and warm place to put a one-year-old. Finding nowhere, I handed him to Ooleesie, who brought him to a warm truck parked nearby.

'Here, take Minnie Mouse, she's quiet.' Danny gave me her lead.

Mike, Danny, and I raced back and forth from the plane to fence posts tying dogs on one by one, out of reach of each other to avoid fights. When they were all secured, we boarded a truck with our luggage to bring us to our house, about half a kilometre from the airstrip. Until now, I hadn't noticed that the plane also carried another passenger, a young woman called Lizzie, who had travelled in the cockpit with the pilot because, like many Inuit, she was afraid of dogs.

Our house on the left facing the beach.

We had been allocated house number 23, a compact wooden structure built on stilts in the permafrost, and identical to the dozen others along the seashore. Despite being bare and empty, it felt cosy and I was relieved to find it had all the facilities of a house thousands of miles further south. I investigated the bathroom first, happy to see a flush toilet and bathtub with running hot and cold water.

'You've been saved from the infamous honey buckets.' Danny laughed, poking his head in the door. 'And here's the water tank hiding behind the front door.'

'Now you won't have to go to chip blocks off icebergs for water either.'

I joined him to inspect the plumbing. Fresh water was delivered by truck every day into this tank. Wastewater and sewage, on the other hand, were stored in a tank under the house and emptied daily by the sewage truck. Apart from a fridge, electric cooker, sink and cupboards, there was no other furniture. The children sprinted from room to room, hiding in the empty cupboards and shrieking in delight at finally having space to play. I almost joined them until I noticed our box of food had not arrived with us. Then, a lilting, staccato voice came through the door.

'Sorry I couldn't make it to the airport to meet you guys.' A pale, young woman with long blonde hair came in, dressed in a white, fox fur-trimmed *amauti*, the traditional Inuit garment for carrying babies. 'But you found the house anyway.' Glowing like a snow queen, Anne Gardner, who worked for the local housing association, came to check on the house. We had corresponded briefly to arrange the rental. This was a stroke of luck for us because due to a housing scarcity throughout the Canadian Arctic, our Canadian contacts told us it would be impossible to rent in any of the communities, but because of its remoteness, Grise Fiord might be our only hope. It was up to the local housing committee to accept us. Our timing was perfect, some Grise Fiord families had recently moved down to Iqaluit or further to Inukjuak in Quebec and they were now looking for other families to replace them.

'There was a problem with the furnace, but I guess it's fixed,' she said, pressing the thermostat on the wall. Instantly, with a roar from the furnace cupboard, hot air blew from under-floor ducts into every room.

'You'll be warm enough now.' she smiled, rocking five-month-old Mark in her amauti. 'I have to go. If you have any problems, call me. I'll be in the Housing Association Office tomorrow.'

'Well … we have one small problem already,' I blurted as she made for the door, 'our box of food is missing. Can I get some food in the store? What time does it open?'

'Maybe about two-thirty or three tomorrow.'

'Tomorrow.' It was only late afternoon.

'I can give you some things, what do you want?'

'Anything you can spare would be great.' Not including seal meat, I almost added.

'Ok. I'll send PJ over.'

As soon as Anne left, a swarm of children arrived. Awkward and shy at first, they stood outside the open door eyeing our children, fidgeting and giggling. But when I turned my back to unpack, mayhem broke out as ten youngsters raced about the house, banging doors, squeezing into empty cupboards and hiding amongst our boxes, in a game of hide-and-seek to the joy of the younger Osbornes. Like a passing tornado, the boys rushed off to the next house leaving two older girls, Pauline and Susi, to play with Tempy.

While Danny walked back to the airstrip to check on the dogs for the night, a caravan of people streamed through the door carrying a table, two chairs, a bed frame and two large mattresses, all orchestrated by Ooleesie. She carried a box of food, detergent, and washing-up liquid and PJ, her blonde four-year-old grandson, delivered groceries from Anne. Ooleesie, I gathered, was Anne's mother-in-law, I would soon figure out all the inter-relationships in this small, tight-knit community. I briefly met Anne's parents, Mike and Margaret, in Iqaluit on our way here. They had moved to the Canadian Eastern Arctic from England in 1955 as Anglican missionaries and had intriguing stories to tell of their early days here, but I was so preoccupied with sorting our gear, dogs and children that I regretted not having more time to chat with them.

'Hey, what's happened here? Am I in the right house?' Danny beamed on entering our transformed home. He was just in time for a dinner of baked beans and eggs, all from Anne and Ooleesie.

'Do you remember the other passenger on the plane? he asked, buttering some toast.

'The woman in the cockpit?'

'That was Lizzie Flaherty, seems there's a big family of Flahertys living here'

'How did an Irish name get way up here?'

'I think they're related to Robert Flaherty, who made *Nanook of the North*.'

It turned out there were three generations of Flahertys living in Grise Fiord, all descendants of the Irish-American film-maker Robert J. Flaherty, who travelled to Northern Quebec from the US in the early 1920s to make the famous docudrama *Nanook of the North*, portraying the hunting life of an Inuk man and his wife. Maggie Nujarluktuk, who played the young woman, was five months pregnant with Flaherty's child when he finished filming and returned to his wife and children in the US to continue his movie career. He had no further contact with her or his son, Josephee, who was Lizzie's father. Flaherty's film was an international success, but his true Arctic legacy, I discovered, is his Inuit descendants, who continue to thrive and contribute to modern Inuit society today.

'There's so much to learn about this place, but right now, we need to get the kids to bed.' I herded them into the bathroom, found their toothbrushes and popped Orla on the toilet. 'Uh-oh we have no toilet paper or tissues.' I called to Danny.

Minutes later, Ooleesie appeared at the door again, waving two rolls over her head with a flourish. Who needed language when you could use telepathy?

Chapter Two

I woke early to a hushed house taking a few seconds to register where I was, but the view through the small bedroom window left me in no doubt. A spotless mantle of soft snow smothered the tundra and piled into drifts where the wind had pushed it against sheds. Hunks of moored ice appeared as phantom boats docked at the water's edge, only metres from the house. Parked snowmobiles, sledges and boxes, all cloaked in snow, were enchanting spectral forms in the grey dawn light. This was our new world, our new life for the next year. I lay back in the bed to savour the anticipation.

Thoughts of how all this came about trickled back. Nine years previously, when I was a medical student living in Dublin, my friend Sheila told me her boyfriend John, a team member of the First Irish Arctic Expedition, was packing expedition equipment for their exploration of north-west Ellesmere Island, in a small warehouse off Camden Street near where I lived at the time. In need of distraction on a wet Sunday afternoon, I popped in to volunteer assistance, and there I met Danny, who introduced me to the small world of art in Ireland as well as travel to the remote Canadian Arctic. Although I was never a thrill-seeker, I was attracted to his adventurous spirit. We met again after he returned from his arctic expedition and a year later, when I had qualified in medicine and was working as a junior hospital doctor, we married and started planning our own travels. 'We need to do these things now,' he would often say to me, 'because life is short.'

'But we're still young.' I would reply, thinking his perception of our mortality had been influenced by the early deaths of his immediate family. He was born and grew up in the south of England. His father, a RAF pilot was killed in a plane crash when Danny was only seven years old, and he was then sent off to boarding school for the next eleven years of his life, which he hated. His only sibling, Kay, who had been ill for years, died of renal failure when she was in her teens, and his mother passed away from cancer a year before I met him. All deeply traumatic events for a young person to deal with on their own. In converse, my Irish upbringing involved my parents, five lively siblings, a benevolent grandmother, aunts and uncles with dozens of cousins and friends, who were all an important part of my life.

Danny moved to the Beara Peninsula in 1971 and after we married, I moved there too. We continue to live here, but he always remained captivated by the Arctic wilderness, the wide-open spaces, the lifestyle, and the opportunities, especially for going out on the land and painting. He yearned to go back, and although I was keen to see the place he was so smitten with, I first wanted to go somewhere less cold, like South America, which piqued my curiosity. We opened 'South America' in our atlas on the kitchen table, looked for the highest concentration of volcanoes there and hatched a plan to traverse down the middle of the Andes between Chile and Argentina for six months, alone, apart from buying llamas to carry our gear. But we had a big problem. I became pregnant well into our planning process, by which time commitments were made, such as making a film of our journey for RTÉ, and money had been spent. I didn't see a way out. Our first baby, Tempy, was born three months before our departure, and I could not bring her because of the effects of altitude and other dangers on the journey, even deferring our travel would not solve this problem. Heartbroken, I left her behind with my mother, but knowing how besotted she was with her first grandchild eased some of the pain of the separation. I had been hard on myself, suppressing my emotions to achieve our goal. Three years later, after

Orla was born, we left both children with my sister when we joined the Irish North Peak of Everest climbing expedition to Tibet, a shorter time away. Still, we knew we could never leave them behind again, even though my family gave them the best care possible during our absence.

Now was the right time to go somewhere cold, where our entire expedition centred around the children, taking them to a place where other youngsters were already thriving and planning a journey that was suitable for them. Occasionally, small seedlings of anxiety emerged when I pondered the hazards of a journey to Greenland, but I didn't let them grow. Danny was excited when he came across the story of the last Inuit migration to Greenland and was convinced that retracing this migration was achievable for us. And having experienced the rigours of travelling on the ice of Ellesmere Island, he was familiar with the terrain and the risks involved, whereas I could only let my imagination run wild.

'They'll be fine', he insisted whenever I voiced my concerns for the safety of the children. 'We'll make sure they're warm and protected. Anyway, children here travel on the ice with no problem.'

I needed to find out more about this polar migration. While he pored over detailed maps searching for the best route for our journey, I researched reports of the Qitdlarssuaq saga. Inuit history comes from an oral tradition and various fragments have been documented from different sources years after the event. A French missionary priest and anthropologist, Guy Mary-Rousseliere, who spent fifty-six years living in the Canadian Arctic, wrote the most detailed and cohesive narrative. The story began somewhere near Igloolik in the mid-nineteenth century when a shaman or *angakkuq*, called Qitdlarssuaq, had a vision of people living further north but completely cut off from the rest of the world. He convinced a group of about forty Inuit to follow him to find these people. As an *angakkuq*, a mediator between the human and spirit world, he possessed strong powers of persuasion, but another version of the story tells us that Qitdlarssuaq, with his companion Oqi, murdered a man and although a motive for their crime was not clear, a vendetta was being pursued against them by the victim's family and friends. During a revenge attack, while they were out hunting, they managed to repel the assailants with bow and arrows from a vantage point on top of a nearby iceberg, but Qitdlarssauq knew they would be back and the only way to escape was to go somewhere distant and unknown. Enlisting family and friends, including Oqi, he formed a group of followers, men, women and children, to travel further northwards from the north of Baffin Island across Lancaster Sound to Devon Island. This was a hazardous crossing, the sea ice continuously fractured and moved, forcing them to make many detours for better conditions. Progress was slow. Their sledges or *qamutiit* pulled by dogs were heavily laden with all their belongings, including kayaks. and they had to make camp several times on the pack-ice.

Contemplating the perils of travelling across moving ice and relieved we would not be doing that first part of the journey across Lancaster Sound, I fell back to sleep, to be woken hours later by the excited shouts of children outside. Tempy had never seen snow before, and she pushed a chair to the window to watch her new friends running around, pulling small sledges or *qamutiit*, building snowmen, and throwing snowballs. Impatient to join in the fun she quickly dressed and bolted out the door. I brought Orla out into the crisp, cold air to see her sister being ferried around in a small *qamutiik* by two boys. She tried to run after them, but her toddler's legs wobbled on the slippery snow and she fell face down into the cold, wet stuff that would be with us for the next nine months, blowing about in blizzards, collecting in snowdrifts and covering everything with a white layer of frosting. Even though the temperature was only zero, about as high as it gets at this latitude in September, we retreated to the warmth indoors.

'I'm off to search for our sea-lift boxes,' Danny said passing us as we entered the dark porch, 'and I'll move the dogs nearer to the house too'

The annual 'sea-lift' had arrived in Grise Fiord about a week before us, which was fortuitous, considering the large ice floes that drifted onto the beach during the night, and apparently were piled up for six kilometres out to sea. Originating in Montreal, the ship travelled to northern communities, delivering a year's supply of non-perishable goods for the store and households, as well as building materials and thousands of gallons of fuel for heating and electricity. This is a vital service for such isolated people due to the high cost of air freight and is dependent on favourable sea ice conditions; some years, it can't get in to make its delivery if its path is blocked by a build-up of floating ice. Because of insufficient time and funds, before we left home, we had only managed to arrange to 'sea-lift' a small crate containing plaster and clay for Danny's sculptural work, as well as wood which he intended to use to make our *qamutiik*, and most essential, warm winter clothes. Our budget was tight. Funding for a film of our journey that we had planned to shoot fell through just days before our departure, so apart from some small savings and a bank loan, the only money coming in would be from an occasional newspaper article that I arranged to send back to the *Sunday Tribune* newspaper in Ireland, as well as the possible sale of a few of Danny's paintings. It wasn't nearly enough, but that could be dealt with later when we would get a better idea of our options.

Danny arrived back after some hours. 'I had to walk the dogs two by two from the airstrip to the other side of town, over there beyond the last house.' he said hanging his jacket on some hooks near the door. 'It took four trips, but I found a good spot where I chained them on some rough ground near another dog team.'

'Did you find our sea-lift boxes?' I wanted to wear our winter clothes.

'I didn't make it there, I'm afraid, because our biggest problem now is to get more chain.'

'I thought you brought enough of it in your hand luggage? I watched Oisín take unsteady steps towards his father. At twelve months old he was becoming more confident with his walk. 'We really need our winter clothes now, especially for the kids'

'Well, the chain is our priority now, we don't have enough to tie all the dogs out securely.' He put the kettle on for tea. 'And the only other person with a dog team here is Larry Audlaluk, you know him, he lives in the first house? But anyway, he has no spare chain, and I tried in the Co-op too, but they have none.'

'What are we going to do? How will you get more?'

'I'll have to ask around. Someone might have some to spare. I see other dogs chained up outside houses, mixed breeds, mainly German Shepherd … They're not used for pulling sledges. They just stay chained up outside.' He got the Red Rose teabags out of the cupboard and some hard-tack pilot biscuits.

'What do you think is the most precious delivery the sea-lift makes here?'

'Haven't a clue. Fuel, I guess.' I humoured him while trying to figure out how I could retrieve that important box of clothes now that his priorities were different to mine

'No, Pepsi! He laughed. 'I met some very happy people carrying crates of pop home. They haven't had any in the last month or so, and the whole community is craving Pepsi or C-Plus.'

'That's fuel too – a different kind,' I smiled. His distraction worked and I set about checking our bare cupboards to see what we could use for lunch.

Having eaten fried egg sandwiches, we went to the Inuit Co-op, the only store on Ellesmere Island, a warehouse with a supermarket, open for about two hours every day. Along with a food section, it stocked clothes, utensils, furs, guns, ammunition, and even a post office. Everything a northerner would need was here. I had been forewarned prices were high, very high, and some items were four times the amount I was used to paying. Paring my long list down, I browsed the nonperishable food shelves, pleased to see tinned fish, baked beans, peas, dried sultanas and milk powder, all shipped up by sea-lift were a lot cheaper than airfreighted goods. Fresh vegetables comprised a few onions, potatoes and sad carrots.

'You need to come just after the plane arrives with the fresh food. They sell out fast.' Cecil, the easy-going laconic store manager, told me when I enquired about the availability of eggs and fresh fruit and vegetables. He packed our food, pots, pans and broom into cardboard boxes and didn't mention the damage our dogs did to the food on the plane. Waiting behind us to pay for his box of bullets, a chatty young man introduced himself and, seeing our sizeable load of shopping, offered to deliver the boxes to our house. Oodilatitat was the driver of the garbage collection truck, he told us, so I guessed he hadn't much to do anyway, with only about thirty buildings to service and a kilometre of drivable dirt road stringing them together. For most of the year, this road is covered with hard-packed snow which becomes smooth and glassy with wear. Four-wheel drive vehicles were restricted to this route, but every family had a snowmobile or 'skidoo' that had replaced dog teams as the main mode of transport decades ago. Leaving the Co-op, the hum of their engines and the smell of gasoline fumes filled the air as people started using them again to go shopping, to school or wherever the snow now gave them access. With a rubber track instead of wheels for the uneven icy terrain, they climbed steep hills and zoomed between houses. It would take another month before the sea freezes, allowing skidoos to crisscross its surface.

'We could check on our sea-lift crate on the way home now that our shopping is being delivered,' Danny suggested.

'Where exactly is it'

'Down on the beach towards the RCMP station, it's not far.'.

The plywood crates were brought to shore from the ship by a barge during high tide and deposited on the beach to be collected by their owners. There weren't many left when we arrived. At first, we could see no sign of ours, then Danny found it among a pile of discarded empty crates. He loosened the wooden top with his Swiss army knife enough to peer inside.

'I can see the wood and the box of plaster, but no sign of the clothes box,' he said.

'You're joking.' I put Oisín down on the ground and pushed beside him to look in.

'The most important box is missing. The kids really need those down-filled jackets now.' I glanced at wind-whipped, rosy-cheeked Orla and Tempy wearing light windproof jackets over wool sweaters, barely adequate at -5°c. With the temperature dropping every day, they had to wear something warmer.

'Don't worry they'll turn up. I'll call the sea-lift company,' he said.

'And another thing, I can't keep carrying Oisín in my arms, he's much too heavy. I need an *amauti*.'

The women all wore practical and elegant *amauti*, which were used to carry babies and toddlers in a large pouch at the back, keeping them warm in all weathers. Decoratively trimmed with fur and colourful braiding, they came in two styles: short with a full skirt or long with an apron front and a longer 'tail apron' at the back.

'Why don't you ask someone to make one for you? They have rolls of material in the Co-op.'

'Yeah. I'll ask around and see if I can find somebody. It might be expensive, but I have to get one.'

Meandering along the shoreline on our way home, the girls ran around playing among small, stranded ice floes scattered on the beach. Further on, near Larry's house the sea was stained crimson.

'Look Ger, I think that's a beluga.' Danny pointed towards a white mound beside Larry's canoe. 'Let's go and see.'

'Well … okay.' I would have preferred to see the small whale alive. The blood was off-putting, the children were becoming fractious, and a biting cold numbed my face and hands.

'They were called 'Sea Canaries' by sailors years ago, because of their high-pitched cry,' he told me as we walked down to the carcass. 'You can even hear it out on the ice near open water, like a *polynya*.'

Looking at the Disney cartoon face still smiling sweetly, I shuddered.

'I'll never get used to all this butchering.'

'You will,' he laughed.

'I know. I'm being hypocritical. Factory farming is far crueller and revolting.'

Suddenly, without even a warning whimper, Orla screeched. She had enough and knew the best way to galvanise her parents into action was to yell at the loudest, highest pitch possible, not melodic like a canary. Three minutes later, we were back in our warm home.

Chapter Three

Gazing out the south-east-facing kitchen window, watching the pale dawn sun crown an iridescent horizon, I saw a thin bearded man with long, dark hair and round glasses pulling up on his skidoo outside the steps to our house.

'There's someone coming,' I turned to Danny. 'He looks like an Inuk John Lennon except for that rifle slung over his shoulder, and the big seal carcass he's towing. Do you know him?'

He peered through the window. 'That's Jaypetee, the mayor. Anne's husband,' and rushed out the door to greet him.

'You want seal?' Jaypetee asked, unhitching his load.

'Great! Thanks, that'll keep the dogs going for a while.' Danny helped untie the ropes securing the seal to a qamutiik and dragged it across the snow to the doorstep. 'And we'll have some ourselves too.'

'Sure, try the ribs or liver.' Jaypetee then zoomed up the hill to his house, leaving the seal at the bottom of the steps, while Danny searched the porch for his meat knife.

Living in a remote community of hunters, the sight of dead animals being chopped up was a routine part of life and one that I could no longer have any qualms about as it signalled fresh, nourishing food. Danny performed the dissection on the snow right where the seal was dropped while it was still freshly harvested and unfrozen, watched intently by Tempy, who squatted beside the body, examining the steaming guts as they spilled out through a ventral, midline incision. 'What's that?' she asked wide-eyed, as he pulled out the blood-filled heart, totally absorbed when he described what he was doing. After the organs were set aside and the skin peeled back, he expertly cut out the ribs and 'jointed' the whole animal according to a precise routine that he had learned while helping to cut up seals with dog team owners in Iqaluit weeks previously. As a spectator then, I watched one owner cut open the uterus and extract a small foetus from the seal, throwing it high in the air for his children who raced to grab it as though it was a coveted toy. Nothing is wasted, he advised us. The dogs devour every part of the seal, but the flippers, he emphasised, must be discarded to avoid serious anal lacerations from the sharp claws.

We needed to acquire a taste for 'country food' ourselves. A staple of the Inuit diet, it was available and highly nutritious, so we had to get used to it. For dinner, I boiled the ribs from the seal that Jaypetee delivered to us. The simmering pot's unappetising, pungent, oily smell permeated the house. When I brought the meat to the table to serve, Tempy took one look at the dark, almost black meat and refused it outright.

'I don't want that!' She pushed her plate away.

'What, this is the best food I have ever tasted; it's delicious.' Danny said, cutting small pieces of the meat on plates in front of Orla and Oisín who had no food prejudices. 'Look, your brother and sister love it, they're going to clear their plates.'

'We'll get used to it.' I mumbled picking at my meal, coaxing myself to like this beef textured meat with a strong fishy taste. 'I think vegetarians would have a hard time surviving here.'

When we eventually became more discerning of country food, we found out that this big old male seal, often called a 'stinker' was not the best introduction to eating the species. From that time, whenever Danny cut up a freshly killed ringed seal for the dogs, the type that Inuit usually eat, he would select a piece of the best meat for us, often some ribs and liver. Seal meat, Jaypetee told us, keeps the hunter warm, and when a seal is shot in the frozen, dark winter, after hours of patient standing in the cold at an *aglu,* the seal breathing hole on the sea ice, the hunter pours

Danny cuts up the seal Jaypetee brought for the dogs.

water into the mouth of the dead animal, as a peace offering to its spirit. After this small traditional ritual, some of the liver is then eaten to keep warm. There is nothing like it for reviving the hunter, he told us.

This liver, in contrast to the muscle meat, had a mild flavour, and fried with eggs made a tasty lunch. Although, once, a piece with a peculiar taste had a suspect green sheen, and I accused Danny of being careless with the gallbladder during his butchering. It put me off eating liver for a while. I experimented with concocting recipes for using the ribs and other pieces of seal meat with ingredients I was more familiar with in an effort to disguise the distinctive taste of the meat, seal stir fry, seal curry, seal stew, but it never worked. Inuit often ate it raw, but also stewed the ribs with onions and potatoes, which for me was more palatable. For Inuit who prefer to eat their meat raw, it's full of nutrients, especially vitamin C, otherwise lacking in a traditional diet of scant fruit and vegetables. This was an acquired taste which I didn't manage to develop. Even though I tried not to be fussy about local food, my stomach had limits to novel flavours. Other country foods such as roast muskox and stewed caribou, tasting like beef and venison, were favourites in our house, but not at all as plentiful as seal.

Another staple, sugar, was introduced to Inuit by southern traders such as the Hudson's Bay Company who used it to barter for animal skins, along with tea, flour and tobacco. Tempy had started in grade one at Umimmak school and came home every day with a whirlwind of children who burst into our house, and disappeared under beds, into cupboards and behind doors playing hide-and-seek, pockets stuffed with lollipops after their daily visit to the Co-op store. Eventually, PJ would shout, 'we go gym, *atii*!' a rallying call to move on, and in an instant, they were gone as abruptly as they came, leaving a mess behind as they headed for the community sports hall. Nine-year-old Pauline, Ooleesie's daughter, always stayed behind to play with Tempy.

'Ask your Mom for cookies and hot chocolate', she whispered to Tempy, despite her pockets overflowing with sweets.

'Only if you give Tempy a candy', I bargained, at the same time thinking I shouldn't be encouraging Tempy, especially when she never asked for them. Every one of the young children here had dental problems. One young woman, I heard, had all her teeth taken out and now wears dentures because she couldn't bear the thought of suffering another toothache, the nearest dentist being over 1,000 kilometres away.

Pauline raised her eyebrows in mute agreement to my bartering, one of the most winsome of Inuit expressions, as well as the equally demonstrative wrinkling of the nose for 'no'. This charm was irresistible; I would have succumbed to any of her requests.

In Qitdlarssuaq's time, hunting was the only way for the Inuit to procure food, and although they had been surviving for thousands of years in this way, they still depended entirely on the availability of animals whose migratory patterns varied with environmental conditions. It was a precarious nomadic existence, especially when travelling into the unknown. Hunger and the possibility of starvation were never far away. When they arrived on Devon Island, their fortunes changed for the better, they found plenty of game – caribou, muskox, walrus and geese as well as colonies of guillemots at the end of summer. Devon Island – the largest uninhabited island in the world – wasn't entirely unknown to Baffin Inuit at that time, they went there sporadically to hunt. Today, in our space age, it provides one of the best Mars-like terrains on earth due to the extreme polar desert conditions there and is used by research scientists to prepare for space travel. But less than 200 years ago, Qitdlarssuaq and his people still lived as their ancestors had for millennia. They spent at least five years on Devon Island. The British polar explorer Edward Inglefield (who also named Ellesmere Island, to the Inuit it was known as Muskox Island) records meeting them on 29 July 1853 at Dundas Harbour on Devon Island when he was supplying ships searching for the lost Franklin expedition. They exchanged information via a Greenlandic interpreter aboard his ship, the *Phoenix*. Inglefield would probably have told Qitdlarssuaq about the Smith Sound coast and the people he met further north in Greenland on his voyage there the previous year – important information for Qitdlarssuaq, and more than likely influenced the knowledge he gained from his shamanic trances. Five years later, he also met the Irish explorer, Sir Francis Leopold McClintock, who was a British Royal Naval officer from Dundalk. McClintock was searching for the Franklin expedition and was later credited with discovering the final evidence of its fate which he recounts in his book *Voyage of the Fox in the Arctic Seas*. He also mentions his brief encounter with Qitdlarssuaq's group near Cape Horsburg on Devon Island, dated 14 July 1858:

> The air being very calm and still, the shouting of some natives was heard, although we could scarcely distinguish them upon the land ice. The ship was made fast, and the shouting party, consisting of three men, three women, and two children, eagerly came on board. Only four individuals remained on shore.
>
> The old chief, Kal-lek (Qidlaq as Qitdlarsssuaq was sometimes called) is remarkable among Esquimaux for having a bald head. He enquired by name for his friend Captain Inglefield. The above three families have spent the last two years upon this coast, between Cape Horsburg and Croker Bay. Their knowledge does not extend further in either direction. They are natives of more southern lands and crossed the ice in Lancaster Sound with dog sledges. Since the visit of the 'Phoenix' in '54 they have seen no ships, nor have any wrecks drifted upon their shores. They seemed very fat and healthy, but complained that all the reindeer had gone away, and asked if we could tell them where they had gone to. Our presents of wood, knives, and needles were eagerly received. They assured us that Lancaster Sound was still frozen over, and that all the sea was covered in pack. After half an hours delay we steamed onward …

Whether due to a disagreement or perhaps it was more efficient to separate for hunting, it seems by this time the group had split in two, Oqi with his family and friends had parted ways with Qitdlarssuaq. Tensions are not unusual when pressure rises on an expedition, one of the reasons we preferred to travel alone as a couple. We never used a guide, and even if we had wanted to use one for our planned journey, there was no one available in Grise Fiord to take the requisite long time off, nor could we afford to pay them. We preferred to be on our own, setting our pace and making our own decisions. Nevertheless, navigation in polar regions is challenging. A compass is limited, as the needle is attracted to the wandering magnetic north pole, not the geographic north pole, and at that time, thirty-five years ago, it was to the southwest of Grise Fiord. Handheld GPS units were not available to us then either; nobody had them in the Arctic, and more than likely, there would have been no coverage for our area of travel anyway. We would travel with a map and use the compass while taking into account the declination of the magnetic North Pole, often using a best guess. Traditionally, the nomadic Inuit travelled great distances with a mental map. Completely in tune with their environment, and keen observers of topography and wind direction, their knowledge of the smallest details on the coastline was vast. In an expansive land of limitless white where the horizon can disappear, they used all clues available for direction. Qitdlarssuaq, travelling in unfamiliar territory, often resorted to his powers as a shaman, taking 'reconnaissance flights' during trances to survey the terrain ahead when he needed to decide which direction to take. It never failed him and brought him safely to the ice of Smith Sound and across to Greenland. Intrigued by the unwavering trust and faith his followers bestowed on this shaman, it dawned on me that I was pretty much doing the same thing in trusting that Danny's experience of skiing solo for six weeks through northwestern Ellesmere where the interior had only been viewed by air at that time, would ensure we didn't get lost. He had used 1:1,000,000 maps and an estimated compass reading to guide him, and it worked apart from an occasional minor detour and backtracking.

'Most of our travel is along the coast, and the headlands and promontories are very distinctive,' he said. 'The inland part on the Sverdrup Pass is a long valley and then we are out on the coast again. We won't get lost, even if we get a bit stuck now and then.'

I remembered other navigational challenges we had experienced. For our five-month-long journey in the remote, uninhabited high Andes, along the border with Chile and Argentina, not long after the Falkland War, the only maps available to us were inaccurate and incomplete, with several blank spaces. Every evening in camp, we scrutinised those maps together, identifying how far we had come and deciding on our route for the next day. Only once did we have to backtrack, costing us a day's journey. I was reassured – we won't get lost.

Chapter Four

After several phone calls, Danny traced our missing crate of clothes. It had been unloaded in Arctic Bay, a community further south, but would be on the next flight to Grise Fiord in a few days' time. He borrowed Larry's skidoo to fetch the other boxes near the RCMP station, returning in a foul mood. The wood he had ordered from Montreal to build our qamutiik was totally unusable.

'Absolutely useless rubbish. All the planking for the crosspieces have dry rot, and the main runner pieces are warped and split,' he said, coming in the door and taking off his snow boots. 'It's a heap of shit. I'll have to check out the Co-op now to see if they have any wood.' He opened the fridge. 'I'm putting these rabies and parvovirus vaccines for the dogs here. I got them from Fred, the RCMP officer. They're free for team owners.'

'Well, why don't we use this time now to vaccinate them? I tried to lighten his mood as I continued to fold a pile of clean laundry made stiff as cardboard in the dry indoor air. 'Tempy's at school and Oisín's just gone to sleep, he'll easily sleep for two hours. We can bring Orla with us.' One advantage of living in a small community where everyone looked out for each other, especially their children, was that I didn't need to worry about leaving Oisín for brief periods when he slept. Even though I had reservations about being involved in this task, it would take less than thirty minutes, and it was time I got to know the dogs better. I could only offer occasional assistance to Danny as my hands were full looking after the children. Besides, running a dog team was his ambition, and he enjoyed it. During the Andes journey with our seven llamas, I insisted on rotating our daily tasks to avoid stereotyping roles. But when I looked after the animals, unloading their heavy packs after a long day of hiking, tethering them to boulders and feeding them dried food pellets, it took twice as long, and I never secured them as well as he could. Meanwhile, he had to make camp and cook. Every time I entered the tent, cold and hungry, expecting a hot meal ready to eat, I would find him starting to boil water on the stove, nothing cooked, maps spread out and book in hand. Having eaten, he would go out to check the llamas were secured before getting into his sleeping bag and always retied my poor tethering knots. We soon reverted to the tasks we were good at.

Donning our warmest clothes and taking turns carrying Orla, we went past the last house to waste ground at the east end of the community. A flurry of excitement arose among the huskies as we approached, with much yelping, howling, and snapping at each other. To avoid fights, they were tied to a long length of chain, just outside the reach of the next dog.

Danny insisted that because of my medical experience, I must administer the vaccines. 'You're used to giving jabs,' he told me. 'Inject them while I hold them.'

'I don't know, I've never injected a dog, let alone wild, half-wolves like these.' I was wary of getting too close to the straining, lurching animals.

'Don't worry, I'll hold them securely, they won't be able to bite'.

Walking down the line, he introduced each dog individually to me. *Big Brother*, the boss dog, and *Rambo* his brother who vandalised the airplane, *Little Bitch*, the lead dog, *Jake* who had pulled a sledge to the North Pole on the Steger expedition, *Minnie Mouse*, the smallest female, *Blackie,* and *Fram.* We kept the prosaic names their previous owners had given them apart from one, a white nameless dog that Tempy insisted we call *Ben* in memory of her favourite teddy bear, abandoned by mistake in Montreal airport. An ideal team would have been raised and trained together from puppyhood, but these dogs had never run together, and even though Danny had never actually owned a dog team before, we didn't consider this an obstacle. Unlike me, he grew up surrounded by dogs. As a kid, he helped his mother, a dog breeder, who operated a kennel and grooming business. My parents discouraged us from having pets, so my sister and I sometimes sneaked strays into the house, hoping they could stay, but they were never welcomed. Eventually, in my teens, I saved enough to buy a small terrier, but only a year later, she was run over and killed by a car while I was away. After this disaster, I decided to defer my dog-owning ambitions. Danny loved training animals and learned a lot about running husky teams from the Canadian Eskimo Dog Club of Great Britain before coming to Iqaluit, where he met other team owners who shared valuable information. The dogs themselves establish a strict pecking order, he told me. This was happening, but occasionally, a usurper would challenge another dog's position.

Quickly and clumsily, I stabbed each dog in the thigh muscle with a vaccine syringe as Danny struggled to hold them still. To my amazement, these assaults went unnoticed, even once when the needle inadvertently touched bone and came out bent.

'My God, these dogs are tough, I can't believe he didn't feel that!' I discarded the syringe with the angled needle into a box for disposal.

'They have to be to survive here', Danny said, grabbing the next dog by its collar.

Inuit dogs, I read, evolved from a common ancient wolf ancestor who roamed Northern Siberia about 35,000 years ago. With their luxuriant coats, alert ears and slanting narrow eyes, they resembled exotic wolves, especially when they raised their heads to howl – they are unable to bark, and like wolves, they show predatory aggression, so I kept a careful eye on Orla to make sure she stayed out of their reach. Completely adapted to one of the most hostile environments on earth, they are the only domestic animal of the Inuit and have been essential to their survival for millennia. Now, their use for pulling sledges has been in decline since the introduction of the snowmobile some decades earlier. Before our arrival, Grise Fiord had only one dog team – Larry's. But there was a resurgence of interest in dog travel, mainly due to their value for tourism and sports hunting and perhaps also a recognition of Inuit cultural heritage. The regard and generosity shown to our dogs by the hunters in Grise Fiord was invaluable, because with no dried dog food available in the Co-op store, securing food for them was Danny's chief preoccupation, apart from their training. A hunter often gave him a seal, otherwise he would ask around to buy one. Occasionally, when the children were sleeping, I sneaked out to help him throw meat to the dogs. They only needed to be fed on alternate days as a diet of seal is high in fat and protein. One seal fed them all, and they ate every part except for the flippers.

Danny found acceptable replacement wood for the *qamutiik* in the Co-op and set to work constructing our new dog sledge outside the house, under the kitchen window from where I could conveniently monitor its progress while working inside. At four metres long, it had to be a balance between substantial size and not too heavy, capable of carrying all five of us and our gear across the ice for weeks. Following the traditional Inuit design for *qamutiit*, which he learned years previously in Qikiqtarjuaq on Baffin Island, no screws or nails were used. Instead, he

Danny making our qamutiik.

attached each crosspiece or *napook* to the runners by lashing it on with a rope using a simple knot, which gave the sledge the strength and flexibility needed for the hammering it would get on the ice. Historically, the Inuit used salvaged driftwood if they could find some, since there are no trees growing here. They also used pieces of whalebone lashed together or, if really stuck, even fish frozen together as a plank. They spent time pouring water on the bottom of the runners, icing and re-icing them for a polished even surface. Now Danny only had to attach a smooth teflon strip, which lasted longer and was not so easily shattered. Using a fan hitch formation, each dog is then attached individually to the *qamutiik* from a single point, not in tandem as in forested regions such as Alaska. This Inuit method allows the dogs to choose their own path in rough areas on the sea ice.

'The *qamutiik* is finished, so I'm going to make a box that can be lashed onto it to shelter the kids, like the ones they use here with a roof and front opening,' Danny announced at our lunch break. 'I'll need to get the lightest plywood available'.

But when the box was finished, it was too heavy. He dragged it off the *qamutiik*.

'I have to cut windows in the sides and back of the box to reduce the weight. Can you give me a hand to bring it into the house to finish it?' he shouted to me through the door.

'It's very big,' I was surprised by its bulk. 'It's like an ark, I hope we can get it in.'

We heaved it up the steps, through the front door, and into the kitchen, where he started cutting the windows and taking up most of the floor space chopping Goretex fabric which we brought with us.

'I'm going to cover the windows with this lightweight material, it won't take long,' he promised. 'That'll keep it windproof and snug.'

When it was finished, the children tumbled about inside, using it as a playhouse. 'You're going to have great fun when we bring your playhouse outside on the *qamutiik*,' I said. Although, I tried to imagine exactly what that would be like. How cold could it be? It was too early to know yet.

With our deluxe *qamutiik* finished Danny then announced we needed to buy two more dogs.

'We need to increase the pulling power of our team and allow for any mishaps that might put a dog out of action, like injuries to a foot or leg,' he said.

But dogs were scarcer in Nunavut than he realised. A viral distemper epidemic had killed over a thousand dogs the previous year, travelling up as far as Grise Fiord and even across to Qaanaaq, in Greenland, where up to eighty per cent of their dogs died. It's thought that the disease was probably carried by foxes as well as dog-to-dog spread. After days of phone calls, he secured two male huskies from a hunter in Iglulik. A quiet, grey dog we named Johnny after his owner, and another we called Iglu.

As the days got shorter and the nights began to stretch, Danny started sewing twelve harnesses, using webbing recycled from the sealift sling straps used for landing the packing cases. When he needed advice on how to make them, elders Akeeagok or Tookillkee explained the details of the design and how to measure the lengths using his forearm as a guide. They grew up at a time when dog teams were the sole mode of transport, and everyone used them for hunting.

A whip made of sealskin was another traditional tool to assist with running dog teams, and Danny needed one for our team. 'It's essential to give added emphasis to commands because I still have problems getting some dogs to follow orders,' he said.

'Is that not cruel?'

'No. You rarely punish a dog, just flick it from one side or the other when turning. A guy in Iglulik still makes whips from *ujjuk*, the bearded seal skin so I'm going to ask him to make me one.'

When it arrived in the post, he was surprised at its length and weight and found it impossible to control when he tried using it out on the ice, he almost lacerated his face and vowed to shorten it before trying again. Larry had a traditional Greenland whip that had a longer handle and shorter thinner thong, so he redesigned it, carving a longer handle from Teflon and shortening the tapered *ujjuk* thong. Tookilkee gave him instructions on how to use it, and with practice, it became an indispensable part of his dog sledging gear. 'I don't need to touch the dog,' he said, 'just the sound of the whip cracking in the air is enough to focus attention on commands.'

Filling my days with domestic chores unsettled me, most people had jobs, often part-time, and I wondered if I could do some useful work using my medical training. I read an interesting article published in the Arctic Medical Research journal about a pilot study investigating environmental contaminants in the diet of Inuit in Qikiktarjuaq. This research found that Inuit were being exposed to high levels of contaminants, specifically polychlorinated biphenyls or PCBs, in their traditional food. PCBs accumulate in the fatty tissue of the animals that eat them, and this gets magnified higher up on the food chain and small whales, being near the top, have high levels. The Inuit, who eat delicacies such as maktaaq, the skin and blubber of beluga and narwhal, are at the top of the food chain. One in five Inuit consumed more than the acceptable daily intake, with children and women of childbearing age most at risk. The Arctic doesn't have industries to produce these pollutants. Instead, the source was from industrial countries as far away as Asia. At that time, in the late 1980s, this was new information and there was still a lot unknown about the effects of these contaminants and their distribution in other communities. Country foods in Grise Fiord are from different animal populations to those further south, so I thought it would be useful to do a similar study to find out if they had the same levels of contamination. I presented the project to the local Hamlet Health Committee and the Hunters and Trappers Association, proposing to collect tissue samples from the hunters' catches and undertake a dietary assessment of the families in the community. They were interested and supportive, so I wrote to the National Health Research and Development Program to find out more about their 'Special North of 60 Initiative'. It was lining up very nicely, the nursing station agreed to act as a resource centre to assist with the dietary questionnaire, and the specimen analysis would be carried out by the Department of Fisheries and Oceans. Then, a curt letter from Immigration Canada informing me that my limited visitor visa status did not allow me to do this work put a stop to the proposal. I scrunched the letter up in disappointment. I hadn't considered it to be employment as I was not going to be earning wages. Later, I was grateful for this rejection because I hadn't known then about the unintended disastrous consequences the communication of the results of the original study had in the community of Qiqiktarjuaq. Not surprisingly, the consumption of healthy, nutritious country foods dropped in favour of junk food and rates of breastfeeding also reduced dramatically. Another aspect I became more aware of as time passed was that many Inuit feel, with justification, that they are over-researched. They are a small, unique population of interest to anthropologists, ethnologists, sociologists, psychologists, biomedicine, and the list goes on. But they, the subjects, rarely see any gain from all this study, while the researcher's career reaps benefits. They have been research subjects since Victorian times when the wider public began to show interest in inaccessible corners of the world.

And I had completely underestimated the amount of work involved in preparing for the journey that lay ahead of us, especially making warm clothes for the whole family. Having thrown the terse official letter in the rubbish, I opened a small package that had also arrived in the post. It contained a cassette tape recording filled with messages from my family in Ireland. I popped it into the cassette player, and the voice of my five-year-old nephew Paul asked, 'do Oisín and Orla still run around naked, even in the Arctic?' I laughed, watching both siblings chase each other around the warm kitchen, wearing no clothes.

The nurturing, non-punitive approach the Inuit use in raising their children here impressed me. 'I notice in the south, parents are always telling their kids, don't do this, don't do that, leave it alone. All the time, for only small things.' Anne once said to me. 'Then they stop listening and don't do what their parents ask. Here, we only say that to our kids if it's something important, and then they listen to us.'

For a hunting society, listening to adults is essential for learning by observation and practice which is the way these youngsters train to survive in a harsh environment. Watching and doing with an adult is valuable for teaching children in the southern world too, I reminded myself. But, in our fast-paced lives with both parents working, it's not easy to have that time for our children. I certainly didn't when I worked full-time, but Danny being the home parent filled that gap for me, although I often missed the experience.

Here, young children were with their mothers all the time, tucked up in the *amauti* on her back even while the mother worked at the checkout in the Co-op or in an office. Every woman wore an *amauti* carrying a young child in Grise Fiord, all except for me, and I desperately needed to get one.

Chapter Five

October arrived with plummeting temperatures and shrinking daylight. Thick ice sludge formed around the shoreline, congealing the sea to a briny porridge. In a couple of weeks, it would coalesce and solidify to form a sturdy surface, giving the hunters good access to marine animals once again. While Danny's thoughts were directed towards dog welfare, mine were fixed firmly on securing warm clothing for us all. Housebound, I urgently needed an *amauti* to bring Oisín outside in temperatures of minus twenty while Danny was out with the dogs. Having bought metres of duffle and gabardine at the Co-op store and then failing to find anybody willing to make my *amauti*, I resolved to make it myself, but I needed assistance.

One morning, as I brought Tempy to school, I met Meeka Kiguktak wearing a new pale blue amauti with baby Lisa peeking out over her shoulder.

'Nice *amauti*! Did you make it yourself?'

'No, my Mom made it, she always makes my *amauti*.'

'It's beautiful. Do you think she would show me how to make one like yours? I have the material, but I don't know how to make it.'

'Maybe.' She hesitated. 'You're the same size as me. I think she'll show you how to cut it out and sew it. Maybe I will bring her to your house later.'

That evening, Meeka, acting as translator, and her mother, Martha, arrived at our house. Martha said little but looked at me appraisingly and agreed to the task. Unfolding the gaberdine on the kitchen table and using neither a pattern nor any measurements, she confidently cut out complex shapes, sliding the fabric back and forth whilst occasionally casting glances at me with an astute eye. Watching her chop up my expensive fabric was both spellbinding and nerve-wracking.

'I can't believe Martha can cut this out without measuring me.' I turned to Meeka for reassurance.

'She knows how to do it,' she laughed.

Having pinned the cloth shapes together, Martha demonstrated the stitching I should use. It had to be hand-sewn double seams for the duffle lining, which curbed my enthusiasm, but the outer gabardine layer could be machine-sewn.

Every evening, when the children were in bed, I spent hours working on it, hand-stitching the thick duffle. Then, I borrowed Ann's sewing machine, and five days later, it was finished. I put it on and checked it in the small bathroom wall mirror.

'Not bad,' I shouted to Danny in the kitchen. 'If I don't look too closely at the uneven stitching.'

'It looks great,' he said, coming to have a look. 'Let's put Oisín in.'

'I like the luxurious husky fur on the hood.' I pulled it up to demonstrate.

'You know they say dog and wolf furs are the best protection against cold wind.' He said grabbing Oisín and popping him inside the pouch.

'They have a double coat of fine undercoat hair and long outer guard hairs. How does that feel now?'

'Perfect.' I nudged Oisín's legs to fold them cross-legged at the bottom. 'I'll put it to the test outside tomorrow.'

I had to practice the dexterous technique the women here used to pass a child over their shoulder and into the pouch. On our first few outings, I needed Danny's assistance for this manoeuvre, but Oisín loved being in there and soon learned, almost as a rooting instinct, how to find the pouch with his feet and snuggle down to the warmth inside. The ingenious design distributed his weight evenly, allowing me to carry him for hours without any drag on my back or shoulders. I often wore the outer gabardine layer in the house, carrying him on my back to keep him happy and free my hands to do various chores. He reciprocated by acting as a heat radiator, my own human hot water bottle that I relied upon when the temperature outside dropped below minus thirty. Little

My new amauti *carrying Oisín.*

Orla was at a very awkward age for polar travel. She would have been in the *amauti* but instead was forced to walk by having a younger sibling. At only two years of age, she dawdled, constrained by thick layers of clothes, mitts, hat and scarf. Our excursions to the Co-op sometimes ended in her tears when I couldn't carry her, being already fully loaded with Oisín and bags of groceries. Danny solved this problem by lashing a strong cardboard box onto the small dog training *qamutiik* he had recently finished making, converting it to a 'polar baby buggy'. Sitting in this box, covered with blankets and shopping, she was quite chirpy gliding over the drifts, singing 'Twinkle, twinkle little star' as late afternoon became night.

Living in such a small place, it didn't take long to get to know everybody in the community. There were a handful of other non-Inuit or *qallunaat*, the RCMP officer, teacher, nurse and store manager with their partners, as well as a few construction workers, none of whom had children with them. But over the next few weeks, all but the teachers would leave as another Arctic winter was about to set in, which left me wondering just how difficult the winter would be.

Terry and Mike were the first to move. They called one evening laden with goods from their sea lift supplies, including a small portable TV – satellite television became available the year before we arrived – a bottle of wine, and a plant looking for a new home. Both had worked in many different Arctic communities, and they knew all the residents in Grise Fiord.

'I'm sad to see you go,' I said, 'you've been so helpful to us settling in here. And I'll miss your company.'

'This is a charmed community,' Mike said. 'It's not like the other Arctic communities. There aren't the same problems. People work together and it's very safe.'

'That's true,' Terry said, 'but there are two dangers you should know about, liquor and polar bears. Never go outside the settlement, even to the airstrip, without a gun'.

'Oh really?' I suspected she was overstating the danger, but I weighed up which was the greater threat. I reckoned I could avoid drunkenness, and it seemed hard to get alcohol to the community, or so I thought. Avoiding a polar bear could be a bigger problem. I didn't want to meet one without some form of defence, but I'd never even held a gun before.

Danny agreed to give me some rifle practice. Days later, while Oisín had his long afternoon nap and Tempy played in Pauline's house, we went to the outskirts of the settlement for a quick target practice with Orla in tow. He bought a light .22 rifle at the Co-op, which he told me was ideal for small game, such as rabbits and ptarmigan, and was straightforward to load, fire and reload, but it didn't have enough impact to stop a bear. He had also bought a more powerful 303 carbine rifle, a Polish Second World War heavy-duty model. This is what I needed to use for target practice.

'Hold it still and aim for the centre of the box', he advised after he showed me the safety features and how to load it.

'I'm trying'. The barrel wavered as I attempted to take aim at the cardboard box thirty metres away.

'Stand with your feet apart and make sure the butt is tucked against your shoulder,' he positioned my arms.

Focusing on the box, bracing myself for the loud bang (no one used ear protection then), I pulled the trigger and jerked from the unexpected force of the kickback.

'Wow, that nearly dislocated my shoulder,' I exaggerated.

'You missed.'

'I know. It's too heavy, I can't use it,' I handed him the gun.

'I'll look out for something lighter for you, maybe a 12-gauge large single-slug rifle that would work,' he said, unloading the rest of the bullets from the chamber.

'Yeah, it will only be used to scare a bear off, not to kill it. That would be a last resort, so maybe it will be enough,' I said helping to put the gun and ammunition away. 'Anyway, we're unlikely to need it.'

When we got home, Oisín was still asleep, so I looked up a government-issued booklet on safety in polar bear country that we had picked up on our journey here. In bold print it warned, *it is very important that you feel confident handling and shooting your gun, and that you be able to use it under pressure. Practice it regularly.* Well, I thought, if I were in a dangerous situation, I would be able to use it. The booklet was full of practical information on polar bear behaviour. They are solitary animals, their normal habitat is out on the fiords around open cracks on the sea ice where seals, their main food source, are to be found. Occasionally they arrive in settlements attracted by the frozen meat stored outside houses. There was a section on deterrents and how to bear-proof our camp when we travelled. Most advice related to how to store food and dispose of garbage so as not to attract bears – they can smell a seal up to a kilometre away – as well as avoiding camping on beaches, having ready access to a firearm, and possibly making a trip wire fence around the camp as a warning system were recommended.

'Did you read this,' I waved the booklet at Danny. 'There's lots of scary stories of bear encounters. One happened only a few years ago in Pelly Bay. A man heard children making a commotion about a bear, and he went outside to get his rifle in the shed, but he slipped on the ice on the way and fell in front of the bear and was mauled. Apparently, his son who must have been nearby, shot the bear and rescued him, but he was seriously injured.'

'Oh that booklet … I wouldn't bother reading it. We have our dogs anyway when we are travelling, and they always give good warning if there's a bear around.'

It turned out that Danny was right about dogs being effective early warning sensors for polar bears because a few days later, nanuk decided to pay a visit during the night while we were sleeping, oblivious to all the excitement outside our house. Raymond Mercredi, regaled us with the whole episode the next morning when Danny invited him in for coffee. At about 4.00 a.m. a poker game in his house was interrupted by a loud chorus of howls from dogs tied up outside, he told us. Sure

Tempy and Orla find the polar bearskin stretched out to dry.

enough, someone spotted a bear lurking around outside, and the card players ran for their guns and skidoos.

'I was so close, but just as I was about to pull the trigger Charlie shot it,' he said with chagrin.

'Where did this happen?' Danny asked.

'Just over there.' He pointed out the window towards the ice on the beach.

'It was a big bear too, the skin measured at least ten feet. If only I had pulled the trigger a few seconds sooner.' He sipped his coffee, staring out the window, brooding over his loss of a pelt worth over $1,000 – infinitely better than any poker winnings.

The meat was cut up and shared, we got a piece of the hind leg and I was interested to try my culinary skills with something new. Because it was an old bear, I was told it was probably best stewed. I cut it into small chunks and popped it into the stew pot with onions, carrots and potatoes and after an hour of simmering, I sampled some meat. The flavour was all right, but it was tough, so I left it simmer for another hour, after which it was still not tender. After four hours of boiling the meat still had the texture of an old boot, but at this stage, hunger overcame any reservations we had, and we chewed it anyway. At least we didn't have to worry about trichinosis. Thorough cooking destroys this parasite or worm, whose immature form can be found in infected polar bear muscle, making it safe to eat.

The Inuit have a traditional right to hunt polar bears, which is protected by international agreements. Early hunters, helped by their dogs who distracted the bears, used spears to kill their quarry which demanded enormous courage and bravery, but now skidoos and guns give them greater advantage. A quota system controls the number of bears taken each year. The Inuit Hunters and Trappers Association allocates a number of 'tags' or permits to each community based on safe harvesting levels and these are divided among the hunters. The bear population in the hunting area of Grise Fiord at the time we lived there was estimated at a healthy couple of hundred. But there is no doubt today that the bear population is declining in some Arctic areas and the main threat to the sustainability of the species is climate breakdown and its effects on the sea-ice platform that they depend on for food. The total polar bear population in Canada reported by the Department of the Environment in 2020 is about 16,000, but if our current destructive climate change path continues, it is thought they could be extinct by the end of this century along with many other species.

Inuit women have spent a lot of time sewing throughout the centuries, and equipping my entire family with warm winter clothes kept me busy, too. Terry gave me a pair of perfectly fitting sealskin boots or kamiik. Paper thin, they required several additional layers for warmth – duffle socks inside and sheepskin slippers or mannguat worn over the kamiik usually to muffle the sound of the hunters' footsteps as well as for extra warmth.

Once my amauti was finished, Meeka and Martha showed me how to make these duffle socks and liners for our *kamiit*, and I ordered a sheep skin from down south to make our *mannguat*, a painfully tedious job with no proper leather sewing equipment. From time immemorial, the warmest outer garments for polar travel out on the ice have been made of caribou skin and continue to be used by Inuit hunters. We all needed caribou pants, parkas, and a caribou *amauti* for me, for our journey, but making these garments was highly skilled and time-consuming work beyond my abilities.

Tony, a hunter, told Danny that his wife, who lived in Arctic Bay, could make them for us. The price quoted was hefty, so Danny volunteered to forego his since we couldn't afford all the items. He suspected or hoped that his old down-filled parka, used on a previous Arctic expedition, would still be adequate, although it was beginning to develop a worn look with a waxed jacket sheen from all the blubbery meat he handled. By default, our family was conforming to the traditional Inuit gender stereotype of male hunters going out on the land and female childminders and seamstresses staying at home. I came across a recollection by the artist Pitseolak Ashoona, an elder who lived near Cape Dorset on Baffin Island until her death in 1983:

> In the old days I was never done with sewing. There were the tents and the kayaks, and there were all the clothes, which were made from different skins – seal, caribou, and walrus. From skins we also made cups for drinking and buckets for carrying water. And when we caught geese, we used to make brooms for cleaning with the wings, which we bound together …

At least I didn't have to make buckets and drinking cups or goose wing brooms, even if all my spare time was spent crocheting wool hats or sewing several pairs of mitts, over-mitts and duffle socks, all by hand. Most evenings when the house was quiet with children in bed, it helped to tune in to the local radio as I pushed a darning needle through thick fabric. Community radio, broadcast from the hamlet office was a good way of keeping in touch with neighbourhood news, who had a birthday, who was out hunting, who caught their first polar bear, or who was down south visiting relatives or on a medivac. Broadcast almost entirely in Inuktitut, I listened for words or phrases that were repeated. Various community members had different slots, my favourite host was Larry, who sometimes read, in English, excerpts from a book, *New Land; Four Years in the Arctic Regions* written by the Norwegian explorer Otto Sverdrup, who spent four years exploring uncharted fiords and bays on the south-west of Ellesmere from 1898 to 1902 in the *Fram*, the ship he borrowed from the celebrated explorer, Roald Amundsen. With a crew of fifteen, he overwintered in his second year in nearby Harbour Fiord, and because of the noisy, grunting, pig-like sounds from the walrus herds hauled out in the next fiord to the east, he named it Grise Fiord or 'Pig Fiord' in Norwegian. The official Inuktitut name for the community is *Ausuittuq*, or *the place that never melts*, which I thought was pretty apt at that time, but now ironic, given the obvious effects of climate change.

A memorable excerpt from the book Larry read over the airwaves offered amusing practical advice on hunting walruses from a small boat:

> Walrus-catching is often a perilous enterprise. If you see a great beast swimming sullenly and warily under the boat, and about to turn belly upwards, the only thing to do is to row off with all speed before the irritated animal has time to ram a hole in the bottom of the boat, which otherwise it is pretty sure to do before you know what has happened. And sometimes without a moment's notice a pair of enormous tusks are silently thrust over the gunwale. In such a case you must never fire, or attempt to beat off the animal, but must just seize it by the tusks, and lift it back into the water, or the boat will be capsized at once. Even if you are lucky enough to shoot the walrus dead on the spot its weight alone is sufficient to capsize the boat, and they are not pleasant hosts to be received by.

Larry told us he once had to use this action when a walrus put its tusks over the side of his boat. I hoped I would never have such an encounter because I very much doubted my ability to seize the tusks and lift a two-ton animal back into the water. I hadn't seen any walrus yet, but apparently, there had been quite a few around Grise Fiord in August, just before we arrived.

The calm evenings spent listening to the radio were the most relaxing part of my day, but soon I would have a three-month-long 'night', and I wasn't sure how that would suit me.

Chapter Six

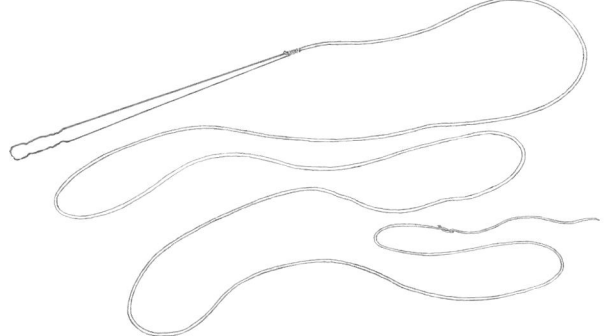

Daylight contracted around noontime, the sun only a glimmer on the horizon as the northern polar regions edged into the earth's dark side by the tilt of its axis. By early November, the sun sank below the horizon and disappeared for three months, bringing the 'dark season' with temperatures dropping through minus twenties into minus thirties. It was such a novel experience for us, but for the other residents, it was to be expected, and no one remarked on it or bemoaned the arrival of another long, dark winter ahead. Regardless of temperature or lack of light, Danny harnessed the dogs and took them out for a run every day. Initially, he attached them to the small three-foot 'polar baby buggy', as a training qamutiik to run two or three dogs. Then he progressed to taking six out on the big qamutiik, doing long journeys of several hours, sometimes over fifty kilometres right down the frozen fiord. On return, he parked them out onto the sea ice close to our house, where he had moved them from the land when the sea froze, making holes in the thick icy surface to secure their long chain. Having tossed their ration of seal meat to them, he came inside, exhausted and famished. I tried to imagine what it was like out there in the dark, cold abyss beyond the shoreline, so close and yet still unknown to me.

'How were the dogs today?' I asked, making a fresh brew of tea as he slumped on a chair.

'They're settling in okay.' He paused. 'There's still a bit of aggression between them. There was a fight before we started today, but I broke that up fairly quickly.'

He started to train Little Bitch to follow commands, he told me, getting off the *qamutiik* to run alongside her in the right direction and then jump back on the sledge as it goes shooting past, repeating this over and over again.

'It's a bit dangerous because I might miss the sledge or fall. Then the dogs would run home themselves and I'd have a long walk in the dark.'

'Can you see anything out there?'

'I don't see obstacles in front of me very well, like big lumps of ice, but I can see the dogs, and I use the head torch sometimes.'

The next day, he got all the harnesses, traces, whip and other gear stored in the porch ready to go out again, but snow started to fall heavily and visibility was zero, he came back and brought Orla out with him instead to check the dogs were secure on their lines. As he was returning to the house, Jaypetee accosted him, 'are any of your dogs loose?' Some children were playing with their young puppy when it was attacked and killed by a big dog. 'You're the only person around with big dogs.'

'No, no, I was just out there checking. They are all secure,' Danny said.

Jaypetee went off muttering he might have to shoot a dog and he just wanted us to know. Ten minutes later Danny heard a shot coming from the back of the town.

Later that day, he heard that a fox had been killed by our neighbour's dog some days previously. The fox's head was sent to a laboratory in Alberta for analysis and tested positive for rabies, so it was little wonder that Jaypetee was anxious. The neighbour's dog had to be put down because of its exposure to this rabid fox.

'Oh, so that explains the shot from the back of town' I was relieved. 'I heard rabies is endemic in the Arctic fox population here, but thankfully human cases of rabies are rare.' Terry had also told me that vaccines are available at the health centre to be given after an exposure that could pose a rabies risk.'

I guessed Jaypetee's worry about loose dogs was also to prevent tragic accidents that had occurred in the past in other Inuit communities involving roaming loose dogs mauling young children, and that, for us, was the main reason we had to be vigilant to ensure our dogs were firmly secured out on the sea ice. All dogs must be tied up in Arctic communities. Sled dogs can be socialised to develop attachment to humans, but that requires early and intensive handling by their owners from only a couple of weeks old and a lot of training. Our dogs came from different owners, with their histories unknown to us. Apparently, this was a problem for many polar expeditions that used dogs – they came from

The dogs tied out on the ice in front of the settlement in the moonlight.

different owners, were not familiar with each other and spent a lot of time fighting. Eventually, when a hierarchy is established and each dog knows its place, a lot of this conflict calms down. Our dogs were settling into their places on the team, and they were also well-fed, so the likelihood of any serious conflict was minimised.

The continuous pitch-black darkness with freezing weather became wearisome. A routine of getting Tempy off to school before 9.00 a.m., then washing dishes, making meals, and cleaning, interspersed with Orla and Oisín's favourite game of emptying all the ground-level kitchen cupboards, gave some structure to create a 'day' in the twenty-four-hour darkness. Once, for respite, when the temperature rose to a balmy minus seven, I brought the kids off to a fundraising bake sale at the school. By the time we arrived there, all the cakes had sold except for a few pancakes and a lump of chocolate fudge, which Tempy was eyeing. But I couldn't bear a sticky mess over them so I bought the boring pancakes. Walking about outside, relaxed in the mild weather while the kids ran around, I wondered who I could visit. Everyone was busily hurrying home after a day's work. Terry and Mike had left, Ooleesie had gone to Iqaluit with Pauline, and Meeka and Iga were not home. A new family had recently moved in, the Kalluk family from Arctic Bay. They had lively young kids and had brought their dog team too, but the parents spoke Inuktitut, no English so I didn't call there. We returned to our house.

In the dim light of our porch, I stumbled over a pair of black boots. Assuming they belonged to Danny, I kicked them aside and barged through the door to find him inside hosting Larry and two strangers for afternoon tea. A tall, grey-haired man introduced himself.

'Hi, I'm Chris Williams, and this is Jonas,' he gestured to a young, fresh-faced Inuk. 'We've just come from Arctic Bay, so I'm dropping off this parcel.'

The children's caribou skin clothes had been personally delivered by the Anglican bishop and his curate on their annual community visit.

This must be auspicious, I smiled, but when the package was opened after they had left a minor disaster emerged. The new clothes, though beautifully crafted, were far too small. Oisín's outfit barely fit his teddy bear and Orla fared no better.

'I should have known this would happen,' I moaned. 'Tony's wife has never set eyes on our children. I gave her their ages as a guide.'

After my initial panic, I saw the situation wasn't as bad as it seemed. At least Tempy's pants and parka fit her, and Orla's were the right size for Oisín. I now had to find clothes for Orla.

Constant darkness and rising melatonin levels in my body, in response to the lack of light, disrupted my physiological clock and made me lethargic. Often around mid-afternoon, when sleep became irresistible, with heavy eyelids and foggy brain, I would creep into my bedroom to snooze, but unruly children, now confined to the house for longer, were a strong antidote to my narcolepsy. And to frustrate me further, Orla and Oisín alternated their sleeping times like sailors on watch, so I never had a moment of peace. The only successful tactic that I used when I felt I could no longer cope was to lock myself in the bedroom, dive under the covers and read a book, cruelly ignoring their bangs and shrieks on the other side of the door. Calmly emerging from my refuge an hour or so later, I would find two sweet, angelic children playing happily together as if incapable of any misbehaviour.

But, if unmanageable children were not enough to make me permanently hibernate in my den, the stink of ripe walrus meat was.

'Tony sold me half a walrus for fifty dollars' Danny was delighted with the bargain meat he got for the dogs. 'He's going back to Arctic Bay, so he's left it in a frozen pile outside our house, but I'm going to bring it in to thaw it out before feeding it to them.' He set up the large metal tub, that he used for bringing meat to the dogs on a table just inside the entrance door where our coats hung and went outside with a hatchet to hack off portions of meat from the walrus pile, returning with an armful of frozen meat blocks which he deposited into the tub.

'You can't do that.' I hated the sight of this big tub of black meat blocking the doorway.

'It has to be thawed out.'

'You know they eat frozen meat too'

'It's much better for them thawed, it's easier for them to digest and they get more out of it. It has to be done.'

As it thawed, an overpowering, stifling stench spread throughout the house. There was no escape from the nauseating odour that clung particularly to the hair and fur on our jackets and parkas hanging beside it.

'I feel under siege by a mound of rotting meat guarding my exit.' I sulked retiring to the bedroom, the furthest point from the source of the offensive smell. 'And it's clear the dog's dinners are far more important to you than my sanity.' I slammed the door and cheered up by indulging in some uninterrupted reading. Strangely, after a few days, I didn't seem to notice the foul smell so much. My nose had become acclimatised, and so it came as a surprise to me sometime later, as I was accompanied to the Co-op by Manasie, a chatty eight-year-old boy, to be emphatically told, 'you stink'. Could this be why we got fewer visits from children now, I wondered. Was 'the smell', strategically placed at the doorway acting as a visitor repellent? It didn't bother me anymore I was now preoccupied by more serious problems.

Our living expenses had been under-estimated and we needed to buy more essential equipment such as a Spillsbury Tindall single sideband portable radio for communication when travelling. Most hunters used them, they worked well in cold weather and it was vital that we have one for safety. Rescue came in the form of a burly, bearded, carpenter from Cape Breton, who Danny invited in for a cup of coffee.

'I'm bushed,' he sat down at the table in the kitchen, 'I've had enough. I'm on the next plane out of here.'

This is not what I wanted to hear from a tough winter-hardened Canadian.

'How long have you been here?' I asked.

'About four months, came at the end of summer. Can't wait to get back to Cape Breton. This place would drive you crazy.'

We were not even midway through the three-month dark season and this man from another cold part of Canada can't stand it. How am I going to cope?

He told us his boss, Sandy, and another builder from New Brunswick were staying to finish off a newly built duplex behind our house and asked Danny if he could help them as they were short-staffed and wanted to be home before Christmas. Desperately short of money, Danny agreed to do a couple of weeks of work finishing interior jobs. On short contracts, the six construction workers came to make as much money as possible, they laboured long hours, seven days a week. and had little contact with the surrounding community. An attempt at integration occurred the very day some workers left. The plane brought in a large amount of alcohol for the two remaining staff, and they invited us to join them for a drink in the house next to ours which was being refurbished. Terry's warning of the perils of alcohol made me hesitant to join the revellers, but Danny wanted to be sociable. We went next door after I miraculously managed to get all three children to sleep. There, weren't many people there, but the vodka was flowing. Raymond, his tongue loosened by alcohol, berated Danny on his reckless plans for the journey to Greenland, especially exposing his wife and children to such risk. Danny took no heed, but I didn't want to hear this conversation. I had been pushing doubts away to the back of my mind, and I didn't want to confront them or have them validated. I reckoned it was better to go along with our plans and see how far we could get before making any changes. It was also apparent this was going to be a long night of drinking, so I excused myself, saying that I had to get back to the kids. Danny stayed, and the next morning, he gave me a fragmented account of what happened. 'Everybody was very drunk, falling about. They were giving us huge cups of booze. Eventually, Steve, the new RCMP officer, came and threw everyone out.'

Life settled into a quiet routine with time suspended in a continuous winter night. One evening – it was always evening, no matter what time the clock gave – Danny went out hunting seal with the Kiguktak family. While I put the children to bed, I imagined a faint smell of rotten eggs throughout the house and thought I was hallucinating, but as time passed, the smell grew stronger. It was unmistakably the sewage. Having checked, I noticed there was nothing wrong in the bathroom. I remembered a ventilation pipe from the sewage tank under the house that went up outside on the roof. While the children slept, I went out to investigate around the back of the house and located the pipe on the roof with a ring of icicles suspended decoratively from the outlet. The freezing temperature had solidified the condensation, forming an icy plug that needed to be knocked off, but it was inaccessible. I had to wait for Danny to return. I went back inside to face the increasingly intolerable smell of the hydrogen sulphide gas. With no way of ventilating it – opening windows or the door was not an option – I went to bed with my nose under the cover, like our dogs who bury their noses under their tails during a blizzard. Danny arrived back two hours later, energised to tell me about the seal hunt with Tom and his parents, Tookilkee and Martha, but first, he got on the roof and smashed the ice off the pipe. I was able to breathe again as the smell dissipated.

'I was riding on the back of Tom's skidoo, going around the fiord in search of an *aglu,* you know those little mole hills of ice that cover a tiny breathing hole for the seal?' he said, helping himself to a plate of spaghetti.

'You peer into it to see how clean the hole is.' he continued. 'If it's sealed off with ice at the bottom, then it's abandoned. The seal scrapes and bites the ice on the sides to keep it open, so if it's very clean, and when you shine your torch, there's water in there, then you know the seal is home. And you wait there, quietly, not moving a muscle till he comes up.'

'That's what I needed tonight, a breathing hole,' I laughed.

Having waited at various *aglu,* they succeeded in getting two seals and went on to Lee Point, where a lead or open crack in the ice also provided breathing space for seals. Danny stayed watching the lead while the Kiguktaks went back to their skidoos to get a harpoon.

'Suddenly, a seal popped up in front of me, but I hadn't established whether I was allowed to shoot seals, so I sang and whistled to it, and it came really close. I had it in my sights but didn't want to shoot it because I didn't know what my position was. The rest were far away, shouting "shoot that seal!" he laughed. 'And I didn't.'

Tookilkee then came and shot it. Tom went to pull it out of the water, but before he could gaff it, the ice gave way underneath him, and he fell through. Danny helped pull him out. His legs were soaked in seawater, but otherwise, he was fine.

'Martha brewed up on the *qamutiik*, so he had a quick cup of tea and I gave him some dry socks, then he jumped on his skidoo and went home.'

'How long did it take to get home?'

'About a half an hour.'

'His legs must have been solid ice?'

'The heat from the skidoo engine warmed him. One trouser leg got frozen, he was lucky.'

A few days later, Raymond also fell through the ice. He was out alone, a long way from town. 'He was on really thin ice,' Danny said, 'as he walked away from his skidoo, the ice bent beneath him and he went through right up to his middle. He managed to pull himself out, spreadeagled on the ice, and dragged himself back to his skidoo without falling in again. He drove home very fast with frozen pants, but he was okay.'

'Now I have another hazard to add to my growing list of dangers to be aware of while travelling.'

'Well, it's still early in the season. There are patches where the ice hasn't thickened yet.'

Not long after, Danny went through the ice himself.

Chapter Seven

'Getting the dogs to work together is critical for safety on our journey.' Danny told me when I questioned if it was necessary to devote hours every evening to dog welfare, after his day's work in the duplex. 'The more training they get, the better they will be, so I have to take them out every day'

I ignored him and continued washing the dishes as he pulled on his padded over pants and parka and exited the house to take the dogs out down the fiord. An hour later, heavy feet thumped up the steps and he burst through the door as if chased by a polar bear.

'What's wrong?'

'I went through the ice,' He threw his boots and over pants coated in ice on the floor.

'Oh God, how did that happen?' I followed him to the bedroom to help him find some dry clothes.

'Larry's seal net,' he removed his wet clothes and sat on the bed to process the event. 'I was on the other side of the fiord, and it was very dark when I spotted something sticking out of the sea ice, and I thought, what the hell is that? So, I stopped the dogs and walked towards it to investigate and suddenly, I fell in, up to my waist in water, hanging on to the ice edge. So stupid.'

'How did you get out?'

'I flung my weight forward onto the fast ice and pulled myself out with the help of some rough chunks next to me.' He put on dry clothes. 'Of course, the dogs were untethered and realised their opportunity to escape. They were about to take off without me, but I managed to grab the handlebars at the back of the qamutiik to stop their getaway. They dragged me along the ice a bit.'

'Wow, that could have been bad. You had a narrow escape.'

Hurrying, he made it home before any vital parts of his anatomy froze. Larry had warned him about strong currents on the other side of the fjord, and he was careful to avoid that area, but what caught his attention and lured him to plunge into the sea was a wooden marker for a seal net that Larry failed to mention. It was a sobering reminder of the dangers of thin ice at this time of year. At least we would not have obscuring darkness during our journey in the spring, and no seal net markers to lure us into open water. He had a good laugh about it later when we visited Larry and gave him a small painting of the accidental dip, made on a piece of wood.

Larry told us how the community of Grise fiord was established. He arrived here as a three-year-old in 1953, when nothing was here but barren snow-clad hills. With his mother, father and siblings, they were one of nineteen families moved to Ellesmere Island and Resolute Bay by the Canadian government from Inukjuaq, over 2,000 kilometres further south in Northern Quebec. They were promised better hunting opportunities, and most crucial, they could return if they did not want to stay – both empty promises, as it turned out. It was like arriving on a new planet for them, they had never experienced such a mountainous landscape, extreme cold or three months of complete darkness before. They were ill-equipped with only canvas tents, inadequate clothing and hunting restrictions. Unable to provide for his cold, hungry family, Larry's father fell into a deep depression and died only ten months after his arrival. Larry gives a heartrending account of those early miserable years in his recently published book, *What I Remember, What I Know: The Life of a High Arctic Exile*. Prefabricated housing was eventually provided years later, and in time, the community of Grise Fiord grew. The people from Inukjuaq eventually moved back to Nunavik in the 1980s, just before we arrived – hence the availability of a house for us, but most, by this time, had decided to stay.

In the early 1950s, during the Cold War era, there were no permanent civilian communities on Ellesmere. However, the Canadian government, concerned by the increasing American activity in the Arctic, decided that the only way to secure Canadian sovereignty was to establish a settlement of Canadian Inuit to live there permanently. This was the true reason for moving families to the High Arctic. Eventually, in 1993, a Royal Commission on Aboriginal Peoples held hearings where the Inuit could finally tell their story. Following this, financial compensation was provided by the Canadian government, and in 2010, an official apology was issued. It was only after the publication of the findings of the Royal Commission that I became fully aware of the extent of this traumatic story; meanwhile, while we lived there, people went on with their lives.

I went out with Danny to help feed the dogs when the children were asleep. Dressed in the usual multilayers, looking like two Michelin men, we pulled on our boots, adjusted our head torches and pushed the tub of stinking walrus meat out the door, sliding it across the snow and down through the slippery tide crack where the dogs were staked out. A full moon beamed high in the sky and the tide was low, tilting the jumble

Tempy and Orla with Bosco.

of ice slabs to a steeper angle. Beyond, out on the fiord, the flat sea ice glistened, and behind me the hills at the back of the house stood out in silhouette in a monochromatic but clearly visible world. 'If only we could always have a full moon, the darkness would be so easy.' I said, holding the tub as Danny manoeuvred it up and over the ice chunks. Living on this dark side of the earth, I imagined, at times, we had been abandoned by the rest of the world, as if we were the only people on a dark planet way out in space where the moon circled overhead every twenty-four hours without setting and the sun would never brighten the sky again.

When they saw us, the dogs jumped, yelped and howled, straining against their chains. We threw meat to each dog in turn, went down the line, and came to Minnie Mouse. 'She's getting fat, I've been noticing that.' Danny stooped to examine her tummy. 'Her nipples are protruding. Damn, she must be pregnant.'

'No, we don't want puppies' I threw extra blubber to her.

'Better to have them now than when we are travelling.'

Later that week, much sooner than we expected, Danny discovered she had given birth when he went out to check the dogs.

'Ger', he called from the front door. 'Minnie Mouse has two pups, it's not good; I think one is frozen to the ice, but the other is still alive. Can you help me bring her into the porch? It's too cold out on the ice. Maybe you could find a blanket we could use for her.'

I located an old woollen blanket that Danny used to cover things in the *qamutiik* and went out to help him get the mother and pup off the ice and bring them into the relative comfort of our cold front porch. While it's normal for sledge dogs to remain outside on the ice all the time, and even if they are provided with kennels for shelter, they seldom use them, we wanted to be sure that Minnie Mouse and her pup would survive so the old blanket made a cosy nest in the corner of the porch. We kept watch on them as they settled in, and the kids were excited to have a pup, a male we called Bosco, and he became part of the family. But he could not remain with us. Jaypetee offered him a good home when we were ready to part with him.

When Jimmy Qaapik, Tempy's teacher at school, started adult Inuktitut language night classes at the school, we immediately signed up. Babysitters were not easy to find as the teenagers were down south at a residential school in Iqaluit, but twelve-year-old Susi, who lived next door, agreed to look after the children when Danny and I were out at the school. By 07.30 when the class was due to start there was no sign of her.

'I guess people here aren't as tied to the clock as we are.' I scanned her house from the bedroom window. 'But I want to get out to this class. I wonder if she's forgotten?'

'Why don't you phone her?' Danny suggested.

After a few rings, Liza, her mother, answered. She didn't speak English, so I had the chance to try one of my few Inuktitut phrases.

'Susitavannippa?' I asked.

I had picked that up from Ooleesie when she phoned me looking for Pauline. Liza responded in a torrent of incomprehensible Inuktitut but I did catch 'siniktut'.

'What? She promised to babysit for me.'

'*Siniktut*! *Siniktut*! Sleeping!' Liza insisted. It was apparent that Susi's sleep was more important than babysitting.

Puzzled, I wanted to protest, 'can't you wake her. I'm depending on her to let me go out', but I sensed there must be a cultural reason Liza would not wake her daughter, so I said OK and put the phone down. Danny agreed to stay at home while I went to the class.

The Inuit, I later learned, do not like to wake anyone while they are sleeping because the spirit or soul is vulnerable in this state, so the transition from sleep to awake must be natural, not done abruptly. They have many taboos and stories, some for good reasons, but others more obscure.

Once, while Tempy was still at school and Oisín was having his long afternoon nap, I took Orla shopping with me in my *amauti*. She was so happy to snuggle down on my back, a rare treat for her. In the store, on the other side of the canned food aisle, I met Larry.

'Where's Oisín?' he asked.

'He's at home asleep.'

'By himself?'

'Yes.' I suspected he would not approve of this, even though I knew Oisín was perfectly safe.

'You know, we say if you leave a child asleep alone, he will grow too big,' he replied gravely, moving off to the cash desk with his arms full of pop and cookies.

Considering this wisdom on the way home, I failed to see any logic apart from discouraging leaving babies alone.

Learning an aboriginal language that was still in use every day was fascinating. I loved the linguistic challenge of different sounds produced by an alphabet of only three vowels and fifteen consonants, although it doesn't strictly have an alphabet. This is a spoken language rooted in the practicalities of living as hunters in a demanding environment. In the mid-nineteenth century, missionaries who needed an Inuktitut bible created the first written form using syllabics. Today, however, a new writing system called Inuktut Qaliujaaqpait, which employs Roman orthography, has been approved by the national Inuit organisation to attempt to standardise and unify the different dialects.

Alas, the Inuktitut classes ended after only three sessions. I guessed Jimmy found hunting more enjoyable than explaining the structure of Inuktitut words to English speakers who had difficulty making the subtle uvular and nasal sounds common in their language. The older children taught Tempy Inuktitut words and phrases and her pronunciation was perfect. I thought I'd pick up some words from her, but she refused to speak any Inuktitut whenever I asked. She had no reason to speak a different language when we always communicate in English; she would only use Inuktitut words with those who speak the language.

In small Inuit communities, invitations to visit are rarely issued. It is expected that you call on homes whenever you wish, and formalities such as knocking on the door are discarded – just walk in and help yourself to food, don't wait to be asked. So, when Cora, the new nurse who had replaced Terry, invited me to visit her at the Health Centre one evening after her daily clinic sessions were finished, it felt like I had been summoned. Although Grise Fiord was tiny, I wondered how she coped with the job, given the isolation and the fact that she was never off duty. She worked single-handedly and had to be available 24/7 for any eventuality with the nearest doctor in Iqaluit, over 1,000 kilometres away. The front door was unlocked when I arrived. I stepped into the well-lit porch to be greeted with a bombardment of notices directing me in both English and Inuktitut syllabics to 'remove your boots', 'put your boots here', on another wall 'hang your coat here', on a shelf 'put your hat and mitts here', on the inside door 'ring bell and wait'. Feeling like Alice in Wonderland, I removed my boots, parka, hat and mitts, deposited them as instructed, and then rang the bell and waited for a response.

'I'm coming, I'm coming.' Cora appeared. 'Come in dear, come in,' she guided me to the waiting room.

'This is a very old health centre', she told me in her lilting Jamaican accent, with a dismissive wave of her hand. 'We are getting a new one and the building will start next year.'

'Doesn't look too bad to me,' I resisted adding 'apart from the notices'. The waiting room had several more stuck to the wall telling patients when they should come to the health centre and the times they should phone, along with more that I didn't read. With only eighty-six people living in the community, it was possible that she needed something to stay busy.

'See that pipe up there', she pointed to a sewage pipe suspended from the ceiling. 'That's where my shit goes. Imagine, I'm working here while my shit travels through a pipe over my head. That's how bad this building is.'

With such an idiosyncratic greeting, I would not have been surprised to join a Mad Hatters tea party, but when she brought out tea and cookies, it was disappointingly civilised. Primary care services in Arctic communities are provided by amazing, skilled nurses who deal with every incident, from minor ailments to life-threatening medical emergencies. I was inquisitive about her work, but she was keen to tell me her life story. Born and raised in Jamaica, she left soon after becoming a nurse and worked in the UK for a while, but she has now been living in Canada for a long time. She complained about the difficulty of selling her mother's house in Jamaica following her death. The Jamaican government would not allow her to take money out of the country, she didn't know what she could do. Steering the conversation back to Grise Fiord, I found out she did not work alone at the health centre as I had surmised. Sipporah, a young local woman, worked with her as a Community Health Representative.

'What does she do?' I probed.

'She works mainly as an interpreter when she turns up.' She cleared away the cups. 'The people here are third world, my dear, third world!'

I took my cue to leave and thought about her authoritative, confident personality as I trudged home in the darkness, past the hamlet offices, then the school towards the line of houses.

'I don't think Cora's lonely anyway,' I said to Danny when I arrived home, 'she doesn't mind setting herself apart from the community and she's quite happy to live in her own little domain where she controls all the comings and goings. Probably suits her job too.'

'Well, don't forget historically most *qallunaat* in Arctic communities were employees of either the Hudson's Bay Trading Company, the church or the government, and in the past, they discouraged their workers from intermingling.'

Over the years, many of the people I met who went 'North' to work knew little about the area before arriving; they were attracted by higher wages or the chance to secure jobs they would not qualify for in the south. As a result, they tended to bring their southern lifestyles. They often socialised together and did not stay long, so there was little incentive for integration. Although this social hierarchy is less evident today, at that time it was quite common. The few non-Inuit who lived in Grise Fiord all held positions of authority: RCMP officer, nurse, teacher, government administrative officer and store manager. As *qallunaat* who did not occupy such roles, we were free from the constraints imposed by these positions, and having young children made integration into the community much easier.

Christmas, a big occasion for socialising, approached, and the Co-op was filled with expensive toys and sparkling decorations that sold out quickly. Close to the holiday season, students and other absent family members returned, swelling the population to 110 people.

On Christmas Eve, a truck pulled up outside our house offering a taxi service to the gym, as the sports hall was called, for the annual Christmas community feast. Sounding its horn loudly, I ran to the window and waved to the driver to go on without us, as usual, we were not ready. The two trucks in the community were busy collecting people. Men in shirts and women wearing dresses and high-heeled shoes piled in, not the most suitable attire for walking on hard-packed snow in a temperature of minus forty-five. We decided to brave the elements. The hall was a short walk away, and we had never considered bringing party clothes, so we dressed in seal-skin boots and parkas. The warm, spacious hall bustled with activity, walls adorned with balloons and fairy lights and in the centre, three lines of trestle tables running down its length laden with festive turkey and ham along with Inuit fare such as maktaaq, arctic char, caribou, muskox and of course seal meat, as well as lots of fresh fruit and salads, specially flown in by Twin Otter the previous day.

When everyone had eaten, the dishes were cleared, the tables dismantled and the fun and games began. David Kalluk played jigs and reels on the accordion for musical chairs, beloved tunes inherited from

Scottish whalers, while young and old joined in with shouts of encouragement and laughter. We took turns passing the parcel, rolling the dice, dancing, miming, or doing whatever the game required. It was 4:00 a.m. by the time we got home. The games continued all week, getting into full swing around midnight when more people arrived. Everyone loved competitive games, and there was always a lucky dip prize for the winner. Traditional Inuit games, developed long ago so that they could be played in a large igloo on special occasions, were included for those courageous enough to try, starting with the muskox push, where players push heads and shoulders against each other, then the knuckle hop, the ear or mouth pull, the knee jump, and the high kick. Even though these sports seemed bizarre, they were very popular with teens and young Inuit adults who wanted to test their endurance and physical and mental strength, attributes valued in a hunting society.

Competitions weren't limited to indoors; outside on the sea ice, seal hunting contests took place. Mimi was the first to catch a seal in the women's event and brought it back to the gym, where it was cut up and shared. The choicest bits, the ribs with a piece of blubber, were reserved for the elders.

A couple of all-night sessions later, I reverted to going early to the games and returning home before midnight; sticking to my usual twenty-four-hour routine proved to be the best way to cope with the darkness. Leaving the house for the gym one evening with the children, I was surprised to see snow falling – so little had fallen since September. Instead, it blew around in drifts, which is normal for this polar desert with very little precipitation. This time, large flakes floated from the sky, landing on our eyelashes and tickling our noses. We pulled down our hoods, removed our hats, and basked in the mild and pleasant sensation of minus eighteen. Such joy this small reprieve gave us! I watched the girls run off, kicking the soft, fluffy snow and vowed I would never complain of the cold again when I returned down south.

New Year's Eve celebrations started with a service in the tiny wooden Anglican church behind our house. Officiated by our neighbour, Aksajuk, a lay preacher, the packed congregation held candles in the darkness and sang 'Amazing Grace' in Inuktitut, while small children ran around boisterously. With so many bodies in a tight space, it became airless and sweltering. Liza opened the main door wide, and in poured a huge stream of frost smoke that went rolling down the aisle right up to the altar as though a holy spirit had entered. At the end, we went outside for a quick burst of 'Auld Lang Syne' sung in Inuktitut, followed by lots of handshaking and shouts of 'Happy New Year'. Jaypetee, as mayor, arrived driving the fire engine and Danny jumped in beside him as he set off the sirens and flashing lights. Aksajuk and Liza invited me and the kids into their truck and we followed behind the fire engine, driving right out onto the sea ice, trailed by a long line of skidoo lights, snaking across the ice of the fiord, finishing with a procession around town.

Delight and optimism were widespread, with the whole community celebrating the New Year and a new decade, looking forward to the creation of Nunavut, where Inuit would have their own government within the Canadian federation and finally control their own destiny. Jaypetee spoke with enthusiasm about what this would mean for the Inuit, when their values and customs would underpin government policies and deliver more appropriate services for the Inuit. It sounded incredibly ambitious to me, but negotiations with the Canadian government had been ongoing since the 1970s for what would be the largest land claim settlement in Canadian history, stretching from the top of Ellesmere Island right down to the borders of Manitoba, Ontario and Quebec, covering one-fifth of the total land mass of Canada. Nine years later, on 1 April 1999, the territory of Nunavut ('Our Land' in Inuktitut) was created.

Chapter Eight

Towards the end of January, desperate to see even a small chink of daylight, I hauled myself out of bed to get Tempy off to school and pulled back the curtains in her bedroom. 'If only I could wipe that blackness away,' I said, disappointed once again to see the endless polar night. But with typical soon-to-be-six-year-old nonchalance, she didn't seem to notice or care whether it was dark or not, just as she never commented on the cold. She had already completed a year at Cahermore National School in Beara and here she was in grade one, learning through Inuktitut with PJ and Jimmy, the two other Inuit pupils in her classroom. After breakfast, we cocooned ourselves in over-pants, down parka, hat and scarf wrapped around our faces like a mummy, with only our eyes exposed, then taking a deep breath, I braced myself for the impact of a sudden change to -35° when I opened the front door – a fifty-six-degree drop from the warmth of the house. But she never remarked on the cold and it dawned on me that she had adapted to life here better than I had, it was a familiar part of the day for her.

The school was only a five-minute walk away, and she asked to go herself, but the heavy front door was difficult to open. I didn't want to risk having her wait outside in those temperatures for someone to notice she needed to be let in. As a compromise, she came home alone, accompanied by other kids. The invigorating wake-up walk was just what I needed to start my day. En route, we regularly met Ooleesie's husband, Gamaliel or Akeeagok as he was usually called. He always seemed to be up early, tinkering away with his hunting gear at his shed on the shoreline. Without fail, he greeted us with a smile. Ooleesie loaned me a book, *The Long Hunt*, written by the photographer Fred Bruemmer, recording an extraordinary journey he went on with Akeeagok and his brother, Akpaliapik, in the 1960s. They travelled with two dog teams, covering over 2,000 kilometres in six weeks, hunting polar bears, caribou and seals, often in blizzard conditions. Now, decades later, Akeeagok continued to hunt in this land he knew so well, but not with dogs, and I wondered if he ever felt nostalgia for the old ways of hunting. Probably not. Inuit are pragmatic and skidoos have made hunting more efficient. But the atmospheric black and white photographs in the book showing the dogs in action attest to a more daring bygone time, even though life was hard then. Bruemmer noted the Inuit and *Qallunaat*'s differing attitudes towards the travails of Arctic travel. He says *Qallunaat* regard Arctic travel as 'a form of personal combat with an alien, hostile environment' and dramatise the challenges, whereas for Inuit this is their homeland, obstacles are to be expected and there is no point in getting annoyed. I resolved to cultivate that mindset for our journey. What's the point of being annoyed with natural phenomena beyond your control? But I knew deep down that I would always respond like the *Qallunaaq* I am.

Around midday, I checked again to see if there was a tiny suggestion of sun showing, although it would not appear until early February. By afternoon, more people were out and about, especially when the Co-op store was open, and to avail of the opportunity to socialise, I made a daily excursion there to buy food. On a typical day, I would pass Tookilkee doing his delivery in the water truck. Apart from a greeting, a lack of Inuktitut meant I never had a conversation with him either. I would see his son Jopee too, with the sewage truck attaching a hose to a house to suck out the sewage. Father filling tanks and son sucking out the waste matter, servicing all the houses. Then, around a corner, I would spy the fuel truck filling tanks to ensure everyone had enough oil to heat their homes. To run out of oil here would be an enormous disaster because it wouldn't take long for every pipe to freeze up. Outside the store, I met Pijamini, an elder who stopped to speak with me. 'You happy?' he asked, with a concerned expression.

'Yes, of course' I smiled, surprised and a bit irked by his question, and proceeded to the warmth of the Co-op. Do I go around frowning, I wondered? Or perhaps he expected me to be depressed in the endless darkness, and maybe I was suffering from SAD – seasonal affective disorder. The more I thought about this, I realised the darkness was having a big effect on me. I struggled with lethargy, irritability and low mood. Two nights previously, I was so annoyed with Danny; everything he said seemed ridiculous and needed an argumentative response.

'The best thing about travelling with dogs is that they don't break down, unlike skidoos,' he mused, watching through the window as Tookilkee and Tom took off on a hunting trip on their skidoos.

'That's just an excuse for having dogs,' I said, continuing to hang washing on an indoor line that also acted as a humidifier in the incredibly dry atmosphere of this polar desert.

'No really, think about it. Compared to a skidoo they are much more reliable. Especially for someone with no mechanical skills, like me.'

'Come on, you love training animals. You couldn't be happier than when you are out with those dogs. You're always out with them. You never help with the children or any domestic chores. I have to do it all.' I whisked the laundry basket away and put it in a cupboard.

'Well, our lives will depend on those dogs. They have to work perfectly as a team. I need to put in a lot of time to make sure that happens. So, I'd better get going now and take them out.'

I didn't acknowledge his departure as he left and went to bed about midnight, by which time he would normally be back, but there was no sign of him returning, so I thought he must be out extra far. Probably he is delaying coming back because I'm in a bad mood, well I am fuming with him so he should stay out, then I went straight to sleep. I woke at about 7.00 a.m. and slid my leg over to his side of the bed, but made no contact; I flung my arm out to his side, but he wasn't there. I got up to see if he was in the kitchen, though the house was silent.

Something was wrong; he had been gone far too long. I went over to the window, searching the pitch-black darkness for any movement on the ice outside where the dogs were usually parked, but there was none. He must have had an accident, my mind raced. Could he have fallen through the ice? He wouldn't get lost; I didn't even know where he had planned to take the dogs. I wasn't sure what to do. Should I call the RCMP station? With mounting alarm, I decided to call Jaypatee to ask for his advice. As I quickly dressed, I heard heavy footsteps climbing the steps to the front door, and Danny stumbled in, exhausted.

'Where were you?'

'Those bloody dogs ran away when I was miles out.' He collapsed into a chair, taking his boots off.

'Tell me what happened.' Relief at seeing him again gave way to guilt for being so bad-tempered when he left. 'I'll make some tea.' I put the kettle on.

'I was right down at the end of the fiord, about ten miles away. I'd turned for home, but their traces were a mess, so I had to stop to untangle

Going shopping in the dark.

them. It takes a long time to do each one, so anyway, the *pituk* broke, you know the piece that attaches them to the *qamutiik*. They ran off still tied to each other, and I was left standing there with the *qamutiik* and no dogs.'

While I dropped Red Rose tea bags into cups on the table, I visualised the horror of seeing the bunch of dogs sprinting off, abandoning the *qamutiik* to the cold darkness,

'I had to walk using my head torch, hoping I would find them,' he continued. 'I knew they would head for home. So, after hours of walking with my torch fading, I picked out eight shining pairs of green eyes in the blackness. Not a sound from them.'

'I'm amazed you found them.' I poured the boiling water into the cups.

'They were tangled around a big lump of ice and were too exhausted to fight.'

'How did you get them back here?'

'I had to walk them back to the *qamutiik* to tie them onto it.'

As we drank our tea, I never admitted to him that I had wanted to run away that night, too.

Although the dogs were demanding, they were getting familiar with each other and working better as a team. Trips when everything went smoothly were becoming more frequent,

'We got off to a good start, no fighting. I managed to get Ben hitched up without him chewing his harness.' Danny said on return from a particularly memorable journey. 'We went off at a terrific speed. It's so cold out there, at least minus forty-five. I noticed a dull glow in the sky, and as soon as we got outside of town, away from the lights, I could see it was the Aurora Borealis, it was just wonderful.'

He told me they started as a curtain over Grise Fiord, which faded away and then reappeared to the south, covering the whole sky with big drapes and curtains.

'The dogs were going at a tremendous pace,' he continued. 'I had to keep an eye open for the great lumps of ice the runners were slipping into every now and then, so I had to keep the head torch on quite a lot, but I turned it off to have a look at the sky, and they were splendid. They were going overhead of me all the time, a lovely green one like a big squiggle, a giant scribble in the sky. It got bigger and bigger and then developed into a curtain. Marvellous!'

He travelled most of the way back without a torch, just watching the displays in ecstasy.

The next night, they were there again, and he took Tempy down to the dogs to see them. They went far enough away from the village lights to get the best view and met Jopee going out to hunt on his skidoo. 'Whistle, suck in your breath, that makes them come lower and lower,' he advised. 'Then bang hard on the side of the *qamutiik*, with a piece of wood to make them jump up again. All Inuit know this.' When he was young, his mother would tell him if he went outside in the Northern Lights, they would come down and chop his head off. 'But we used to go out anyway, whistle at them, and bang things. They'd come down and we'd run inside quickly.'

Aqsarniit, as the Inuit call the Aurora Borealis, were rare enough at this high latitude of seventy-six degrees north. Further south, around the sixtieth parallel, the Arctic Circle, is the best area for seeing them, but at times of intense solar activity, when lots of charged particles from the sun excite gases in the ionosphere, they can be seen outside their normal range, even as far south as Ireland. Danny was so impressed by these celestial displays, he made a painting of them on one of the sheets of vellum or calfskin that arrived from Ireland by post from the poet Theo Dorgan, with an invitation to submit a piece of art on the vellum for the Great Book of Ireland, *Leabhar Mór na hÉireann*. This project, a fundraiser for two charities, resulted in a modern manuscript with original work from prominent visual artists, poets and even composers. A patron purchased it for University College Cork, where it is housed in the library and includes Danny's two Grise Fiord paintings on the vellum, which he considered fitting as so much of Inuit traditional life centres around the use of animal skins – for clothes, boots, ropes, bags and other containers.

At last, on 9 February, the first sliver of light from the sun's rays after a three-month absence appeared on the horizon around midday, briefly and without any fanfare. The next day, I convinced myself it was brighter and stayed longer, and on the third day, the top of the sun popped up, or perhaps it was a refraction of the sun, either way, it lifted my spirits and enthusiasm to continue preparations for our Greenland trip. In the community, daily life continued as usual; the reappearance of daylight didn't cause any celebration to mark the event, even though everyone was relieved to see the end of the dark season. The light extended by about twenty minutes each day, and by mid-March, we had twelve hours of daylight, from 7.00 a.m. to 7.00 p.m. To see from my kitchen window, the jumble of ice blocks heaved up on the shoreline by the action of tides, forming fantastic sculptural shapes glinting in the sunshine, then further out, the flat, broad expanse of shimmering pale blue sea ice on the fiord was a heavenly view that tempted me to go outside. But there was a sting, quite literally, the temperature had dropped from the -30°s to -40°s Celsius. A cruel blow that was hard to reconcile with the dazzling sunlight. Looking for confirmation of this seemingly paradoxical phenomenon, and reassurance that it was only temporary and would be gone next week. I casually mentioned it to Leslie, the store manager's wife, at the checkout during my daily shop.

'It's great to see the sun again, but I'm surprised it's much colder,' I said. 'I wasn't expecting that.' She considered my comment for a while and said, 'yeah, maybe it's a bit colder.'

That's an understatement, I thought, grumpily grabbing my shopping. Why did I ask her anyway? What would she know? I've never seen her go outside the Co-op door.

Walking home wrapped in scarves over my mouth and nose, with watering eyes icing my eyelashes and sticking them together, I smiled, recalling my negotiations with Danny soon after we married, when he wanted us to go to the Arctic. I never imagined people could live in a place where the frigid air is so intense, it hurts to breathe. But this did not keep the children indoors. Around midday, the temperature rose a little for a couple of hours, and was perfect for sliding down the slopes at the back of the town. Tempy didn't last long, she was back home in twenty minutes with a freezing bottom.

'Dogs fight under a heavenly display', *watercolour work in progress on vellum*.

Chapter Nine

With our planned departure only three weeks away, Danny was impatient to go and lay caches of supplies for our six-week sledge journey to Greenland. We would need to replenish our consumables on the way, mainly food for dogs and humans, as well as fuel for the stove. He chose two suitable locations, Sor Fiord and Nansen Inlet, a journey of almost 200 kilometres north over the mountains on the west coast of Ellesmere.

'I can't take everything up there for the caches, so I asked Tom a few weeks ago if he could help me by bringing some boxes by skidoo, especially the dog food', Danny said, shaking the contents of the tent bag all over the kitchen floor, to check they were in order. 'He agreed, but now he's dragging his feet when I try to pin him down to a date. We need to get going now, time is getting very tight.'

'I wonder why he's reluctant?'

'He says "maybe next week", I think he needs his father's approval, or something like that'

'Is there anyone else you could ask?'

'No. He's the best person. He's young, he's not tied down to a job and he's agreeable to do it. It's just I need to get going now.'

A week later, after all the procrastination, Tom was ready to go. He had finally received his father's blessing. We hadn't realised the importance of elder's advice and endorsement before undertaking a long journey. All the gear was ready, the weather forecast was favourable, his skidoo was in good working order, and two days before Tom was due to leave, Danny took off with the dogs, heavily laden. They agreed to meet at the small hunter's hut in Sor Fiord, which people from the community had built, Tom prepared to bring a good load of dog food on his qamutiik. Now we had the opportunity to field test our new Spillsbury Tindall radio which Danny had taken with him. This would be our lifeline should any unexpected events happen during the journey. I went to Ooleesie's house to use her radio to call him. Tentatively, I opened the door, tried not to trip over the scattered boots filling the hallway, took my own off and shouted 'hello' so that at least I wasn't barging in. On arriving in Grise Fiord, Anne told me not to knock on doors, 'no one does that here, they think it's children playing and ignore you, just walk in', she advised. Initially, I was surprised at how difficult that was to do, but Ooleesie, always welcoming and intuitive, pointed to the radio in the corner of the living room. Jaypetee, who was having his lunch there, set up the call for me, and Danny's voice came through distant and tinny.

'It's incredibly cold,' he told me. 'Just touching the tent makes the fabric crack and tear. And I took your duffle socks for spares by mistake which are too small for me, so I have no dry socks to change into, so far I've managed to avoid frostbite.'

Uppermost on my mind was the need to tell him about the visit I had from Steve, the RCMP officer, who came to the house that morning armed with a letter from Immigration in Yellowknife. But my chat was curtailed by the awareness that I was also sharing it with anyone listening in from all over the Arctic. Steve told me our visa will not be extended, and we must be out of the country by 5 April. We had already decided to defer our departure for a couple more weeks to allow the temperature to rise a little. And although we knew our visas would expire, we had deluded ourselves into thinking it would do no harm to stay an extra week or so. We were so isolated, who would notice or care if a small family living thousands of kilometres beyond civilisation stayed a few days extra beyond their permit? Most of the time, I felt I was on another planet anyway, a place where time was elastic, temperatures brutal, and we were completely detached from life down south except for the strong arm of the law, apparently.

'I phoned Immigration and they said you can re-enter again as you are leaving the country when you go to Greenland,' Steve had said to me, pleased with his solution to extending our stay here for longer. 'I'll stamp your passports then, and you can stay until 31 August.'

'But what if it's blowing a storm,' I blabbered. 'It could be dangerous for the kids to travel we can't leave then. Surely it would be all right to stay just another week?'

'You must leave by 5 April' He handed me the letter.

'There's no way we can travel before 5 April. It's still far too cold to bring the children on a long journey.'

'Well, you gotta leave and I'll be checking.'

I needed to discuss this new dilemma with Danny, but not wishing to broadcast it, I gave him an update on the progress of preparations instead. 'Tom is ready to go now,' I told him, 'and I gave him more supplies, including skidoo oil, which I had to get from Steve as the Co-op was out of it.' He had been helpful this time, perhaps trying to mollify that harsh letter he delivered to me. 'And I'm still trying to contact Henning Thinj, you know the mayor of Qaanaaq, for permission to bring dogs into the community,' I added.

Then I filled the silences with petty incidents, wondering if we could somehow speak in code.

'Our little *qamutiik* disappeared from outside the house, which is annoying because I need it to carry cans of naphtha from the Co-op today.'

'It will turn up. Don't worry. You're breaking up a bit, and it's really cold, so we'll finish now, but maybe you can call again in a couple of days. Over.'

'Okay. I'll give Tom a letter for you. Take care. Over and out.'

I called Danny a few days later, using Leah Kalluk's radio. Sitting on the floor, she was busy cutting caribou skins, the material for Orla's parka and pants, when I arrived at her house. Again, I regretted that I couldn't speak Inuktitut and had to use Carol, her teenage daughter, to translate for me. She explained that the parka would have fur inside as it is a lot warmer, but the pants would have hair on the outside being too thick inside for pants. Hand stitching skin clothing is a laborious work but she knew it was vital for Orla to have these clothes and promised it would be finished soon. She then showed me a stunning caribou skin *amauti*, with decorative panels of white and darker brown sewn around the hood, the sleeves and the skirt, creating stripes. She offered to sell it to me, and although it was slightly big when I tried it on, it allowed lots of room for warm layers underneath. It was perfect. I had no idea what all this would cost, expensive for sure, but we had to have them. A few days previously, I sold the caribou outfit that didn't fit Oisín to Annie Audlaluk who had adopted a baby boy, a small contribution to our clothes fund.

In total, Danny was away for two and a half weeks laying the caches. The cold was vicious, and for part of the journey, he had to cross a glacier with the dogs, which proved to be difficult. 'The crevasses weren't big,' he said, 'but it was very icy; luckily, the dogs were tired, and I used a rope around the runners to act as a brake, so we slithered down safely.'

I was becoming more apprehensive about bringing the children out in the cold. Now that we had all our caribou winter clothes, we decided to go on a trial run with the dog team on a clear sunny afternoon when the thermometer showed -32°. While Danny loaded the *qamutiik* and got the dogs harnessed on the sea ice, I dressed the children and myself in multiple layers. Finally, covered with caribou furs, we sweated inside the house and then made our escape to the outside world. Oisín travelled in my new caribou *amauti* and taking Orla by the hand, I carried her over the ice crack to where Danny was getting the dogs ready. Tempy made her own way, being used to sliding on snow, but I had to remind her to keep her distance from the dogs; with all those fur clothes, she looked like a tasty meal. Orla sat safely in the box of the *qamutiik* while Danny attached them one by one to it.

My task was to subdue the whole team during this procedure by flicking the whip over their heads as though a hypnotist, but their barely suppressed excitement was palpable and could explode at any moment if I got distracted. When the children were securely tucked up in the *qamutiik* and all the dogs attached, we were ready to take off. Setting out was chaotic. Big blocks of sea ice piled high by tidal movements made an obstacle course along the shoreline and sent the dogs in all directions. Danny walked in front of the team, flicking the whip from side to side while I followed, holding on to the back of the *qamutiik* to help steer around the big ice slabs.

Occasionally, a dog went the wrong way, causing some backtracking, but as soon as we cleared the ice maze, we quickly jumped on board as they took off like a rocket. Away we went towards the white horizon, thrilled to glide at full tilt over the sea ice. The dog's spirits were high and so were ours. After about twenty minutes, their pace slackened, and they settled at a steady speed, the only noise being the rhythmic rub of runners on ice. Out on the open sea ice, we had an unobstructed view of flat vastness, no hills here for shelter, and the wind was merciless, burning our cheeks. Adding wind chill lowered the temperature closer to -50°. I tried to run holding on to the back of the *qamutiik*, to keep warm, but the dogs were too fast, I couldn't keep up. Danny jumped on and off the *qamutiik* at various times, directing the dogs with shouts of 'Hike on',

I squeezed in between the children to warm up.

or 'Atook', but I couldn't do that either, encumbered with heavy clothes. Eventually, when the pain of turning into a solid block of ice became too much for me, Danny suggested I get into the back of the *qamutiik* with the kids. I squeezed in between the cosiness of their little bodies; it was tight but warm, and they didn't complain. We eventually turned for home.

As soon as the dogs realised they were going home, they quickened their pace. When they could see the settlement, they broke into a gallop, exactly when we didn't want them to, with the ice jumble getting closer. Danny tried to control them with the whip, and I clambered to near the front of the *qamutiik* and found the brake, a large metal claw, attached to the *qamutiik* by a short rope, which I attempted to dig into the hard ice at the side of the hurtling sledge. It didn't fully stick and skittered along, but using all my strength to push it down, it slowed them enough for Danny to jump off and get in front just before they entered the ice confusion near the beach. Now, with the magical whip lashing from side to side in front of the team, they steadied to a walking pace and obediently followed him through the tangle of ice blocks to their stake out chain on the ice.

We had been out for less than two hours, but the unbearable cold made it essential that we change our plans. Any time we met Steve, he asked about our departure date.

'There's no way I'm going to travel with children in that temperature,' I told Danny after we unloaded the *qamutiik* and went inside to the warmth of our house. 'But I've been thinking … why don't we reverse our plans and charter a flight to Qaanaaq from here and then come back by dog team?'

'That might work. Yeah … it solves the immigration problem too.'

'And it would give us time to leave for the journey back when the weather is better.'

We thought more about it. Our new plan had other advantages. It allowed us to tackle the difficult sea crossing of Smith Sound, the narrow channel between Canada and Greenland, first, and this had to be done before the spring breakup season was too advanced.

Instead of travelling over the ice by sledge to Greenland, we chartered a Twin Otter to take us to Qaanaaq with our dogs, *qamutiik*, tent, camping gear, and anything else we would need for the return journey to Grise Fiord. Despite crossing international borders, community links between Grise Fiord and Qaanaaq remained strong. Reciprocal visits were sometimes undertaken by chartered Twin Otters without requiring immigration procedures. Traditionally, polar bear hunters came from Qaanaaq across the sea ice to the Canadian coast, but the RCMP officers, initially stationed at Craig Harbour on the eastern shore of Ellesmere, discouraged this practice, and sledge travel had ceased. It is only 362 km from Grise Fiord to Qaanaaq as the crow flies, but at least four times that for our return route. Larry had flown to Qaanaaq many times and had arranged for us to stay with friends there. We invited him to join us for a brief visit, even though he would only be there for a short time.

Our flight was booked for 4 April, weather permitting, which was still early in the season, giving us time to spend with the Inughuit of north-west Greenland before setting off on our journey.

Everything was arranged over the next two weeks. Bags were packed with fur clothes, tent, sleeping bags, and other camping equipment, then stacked beside the disassembled *qamutiik*, and all the dog harnesses, leads, and ropes were checked, along with the radio, batteries and stake out chains. Everything was in order except for Little Bitch. Our smart, sensible lead dog with a fat belly and enlarged nipples was very much pregnant. Danny had noticed she was in heat about seven weeks earlier and had shut her in a big dog pen. However, the urge to mate was so strong she somehow managed to escape despite being surrounded by a two-metre-high wire fence. Now that she was due to have pups soon, she could not lead a team having given birth, and her pups would not survive the journey. We thought we might leave her in Qaanaaq, but we would have to address that later.

The plane arrived as scheduled on a bright, clear day. Raymond gave us a parcel of muskox meat to deliver to friends in Qaanaaq. We waved goodbye and embarked on the next stage of our adventure.

Chapter Ten

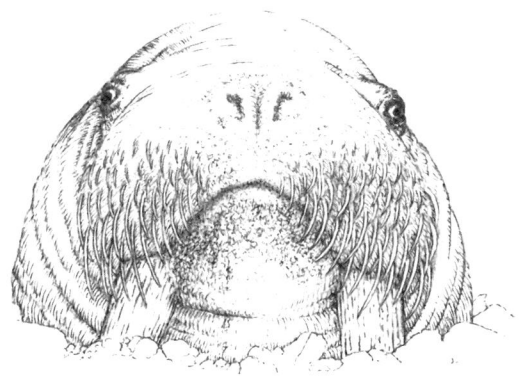

An immense undulating whiteness stretched below us as we flew over the icecaps and glaciers of Ellesmere, then the broken sea ice of Smith Sound to the northwest of Greenland. Land and sea merged into endless snow with no trace of any human impact. Looking out the small Twin Otter window, I imagined myself down there alone, a black dot in that infinitude; the cold is fiercely ruthless, but Inuit have survived in this harshest of environments for thousands of years; this is their world; they are supremely adapted to it. I thought about Qitdlarssuaq and his followers, heavily laden with all their belongings, as they travelled here – up the east coast of Ellesmere over inlets and deep bays that sometimes could not be crossed, necessitating climbing steep glaciers to avoid open water. They persevered, having full confidence in their shaman leader who, during a 'flight', met the people of Greenland. I could visualise them crossing the difficult pack ice further north to where the coasts of Ellesmere and

Greenland are not more than forty kilometres apart. Near Etah to the north of Qaanaaq, they found the remains of deserted dwellings, confirming that people did live there. Caribou and marine animals were plentiful, so they decided to stay in the area and postpone the search for people. But during the following spring, game was scarce and after a trance to determine the cause, Qitdlarssuaq found that the fault lay with his daughter-in-law, Ivalu, who had kept a miscarriage secret. To appease the offended spirits, poor Ivalu was stripped of most of her clothes and left alone in an iglu to die of cold and starvation, but the spirits didn't abandon her. Days later, a small group of Greenland hunters out hunting auks arrived to much jubilation. Qitdlarssuaq's visions had been fulfilled, and Ivalu, by now in a bad state, was rescued by her husband.

And here we were, 130 years later, taking the easy way to Greenland, but we would return essentially as Qitdlarssuaq travelled, apart from a few modern tweaks. This time, the dogs, being more familiar with each other, behaved very well in the aircraft. With no airstrip in Qaanaaq, we came down on the sea ice right in front of the community, having received permission from the mayor of Qaanaaq to land there and bring our dogs with us. Through the small window, I could see lines of colourful wooden houses climbing a slope from the shore and a crowd of people pouring out onto the ice to welcome us.

'Look at all the people!' I nodded towards the window while putting Oisín in my *amauti*, ready to disembark. 'You must be very popular here, Larry?'

'I think it's the plane,' he grinned. 'Planes don't usually land here.'

Many willing hands helped us unload the dogs and our gear this time. A truck drove right out on the ice to the aeroplane, and our bags were thrown in the back. The kids and I jumped in with Larry, leaving Danny to deal with staking the dogs out on the ice. Near the top of the hill, we stopped at a house where Larry's friends, Suulut Rasmussen and his wife, Naduk lived. They had agreed to host us before we set off on our journey. Inuktun a dialect of Inuktitut, is the spoken language here, but Suulut, a teacher, had reasonably good English, which he claimed he learned from

A crowd poured out to welcome us to Qaanaaq.

the lyrics of Beatles songs. Naduk and their two young sons, Angu and Tiki, didn't speak English, but gestures worked well, as we often found. Their house, like many modern Danish houses, was comfortable with polished wooden floors and big windows looking out on enormous icebergs parked on Inglefield Bay. Because he was returning to Grise Fiord on the plane, Larry had to leave with the truck even though it was still early in the day. I decided to go to see where Danny was putting the dogs.

With Oisín in my *amauti* and the girls holding my hands, we slipped and slid the whole way down the steep, glassy track to the sea ice, gleaming in the April sunshine. Bunches of dog teams were tied outside houses, with no sign of skidoos. I had heard that the dog population, the sole means of transportation here, was 700, almost double that of people. The welcoming crowd had dispersed, and Danny was finishing tying the last dog to his chain in front of the town.

'We should visit the store to get some food.' Hunger always made me feel the cold.

'Good thinking. I wonder where it is?' he said.

Truck bringing blocks of iceberg ice to the community.

'Larry pointed it out to me; it's somewhere to the right, halfway up the hill. We could have a look around.'

Orla, not yet three years old, struggled going up the steep icy hill, so Danny carried her. The store, tiny compared to the Grise Fiord Co-op, had a wide variety of European-style foods, including vacuum-packed country foods, and we bought as much as we could afford.

Mattresses for sleeping were laid out on the living room floor, and we tried to be as unobtrusive as possible, helping when we could. Danny dragged large lumps of iceberg up to the house from near the electricity plant where it was stored. Although water was delivered by truck to most houses, people here preferred to use icebergs for drinking water, and chunks of it were piled on the porch. A municipal truck drove out onto the sea ice to the nearest iceberg, where large blocks were chipped away to bring back for the community. In the kitchen, I attempted to help with washing dishes and tidying, but this was Angu, the eldest son's job. I was encroaching on his domestic chores, so instead, I finished making booties for our dogs to protect their foot pads from sharp melting ice fragments.

But, with three active children in an unfamiliar house where everything was accessible to them, it was hard to get anything done. Oisín's preferred playthings were ceramic ornaments, as well as video and audio tapes, which he pulled out of their cassettes by the metre.

'No, let him do it.' Suulut would get annoyed at us for trying to stop these activities. 'You are always telling him what to do. Leave him. He will get tired. He will stop. That's how he learns.'

Surreptitiously, I distracted Oisín, which meant being watchful all the time. Tiki, at four years old, spent hours in front of the TV playing Nintendo Duck Hunt and, after so much screen time, became boisterous. His parents never got annoyed or rebuked him, instead Naduk ran warm water into a metal tub in the bathroom and he splashed and played there, emerging about an hour later content and relaxed.

After a couple of days, Danny was pleased to be invited by Talilanguaq Peary to join a group of walrus hunters on a hunt. In Canada, only Inuit are legally allowed to hunt walrus. Talilanguaq, the Inughuit grandson of Robert Peary, who claimed to be the first man to reach the North Pole along with Matthew Henson and four Inughuit, Ootah, Seegloo, Egingwah and Ooqueah, was small and wiry with a dark beard reminiscent of his famous grandfather. He was a respected hunter and with his wife, Savfaq, Naduk's sister, they made a lively couple. Danny packed a four-day supply of food, tent, fuel for the stove, rifle and harpoon onto the *qamutiik* and headed west over the ice to rendezvous with the other hunters at Naduk's cousin's house on Herbert Island about twenty-nine kilometres away, buoyant to have this opportunity of participating and stocking up on meat for the dogs, but aware too of the risks involved hunting a heavy, aggressive animal on thin ice.

After three nights away, I was relieved to see him back again.

'Everyone was so drunk last night,' I complained after I had tucked the children into bed. 'Lots of shouting and aggression. I tried to stay out of the way and be as invisible as possible, which isn't easy with small kids.'

'Must be drink quota day. I saw Naduk's mother as I was coming up the hill. She was staggering quite a bit. Where's Suulut?'

'He went off somewhere, thank God. He's been drinking again.' I heated some packet vegetable soup I had made earlier that day. 'Now that the kids are asleep, tell me about your trip. Did it go well?'

'It was great. We gathered at Inaluk's house over on the island. Six teams in all, and we broke trail through a light snow. All the Inuit wore polar bear skin pants, caribou parkas and sealskin *kamiik*. They are resolutely traditional, it could have been thousands of years ago. I stayed near the end of the line of teams, and it looked amazing. The light was really intense, with small clouds of mist from the dogs' breath hanging above them and no sound – only an occasional order grunted to a lead dog.'

He paused. 'I'd love some of that soup if it's ready?'

I put some in a bowl while he buttered bread.

Talilanguaq wasn't part of the hunt, he told me. He met him and Savfaq going in the opposite direction towards Herbert Island when he was returning to Qaanaaq. He halted his dogs so they could pass on the trail. Talilanguaq stopped too and approached him, speaking rapidly while drawing a big tummy in the air in front of him with his hands; then Savfaq staggered across and joined in, pointing to a brown dog on their team. Uncertain, Danny suspected that they were trying to do a dog swap for Little Bitch but seeing they were drunk, he wanted to get away. Savfaq's brother, Alo, then drew near them with his team but passed without stopping. Suddenly, Talilanguaq's team took off after Alo, charging towards Herbert Island, but Ani, another hunter, behind Danny, stopped the runaway team and turned them towards home. In the confusion, Danny jumped on his *qamutiik* and sped off. It had taken almost four hours to get back to Qaanaaq, a recent soft snowfall slowed the dogs, but when they got to the shore, Angu was there to meet him, having been dispatched by Suulu, who saw him arrive. They put all the meat onto a rack and then walked the dogs back to their stake-out chain.

'I'm exhausted, but I have to go back down again now to feed the dogs because, for some reason, Angu didn't want me to do it when we came back.' He promised to finish telling me about the hunt if I was still awake when he returned. I waited for him while the children slept and he was back within an hour.

'We followed the coast of Herbert Island through lots of broken ice,' he continued the story of the hunt, 'and, after about twenty kilometres, pulled up beside a tiny hunter's cabin for sleep,'.

They ate tea and biscuits and then spread sleeping bags on a platform, which took up most of the space.

'I managed to secure a place near the edge,' he said, 'but sleep didn't come easy for me with a thunder of loud snores throughout the night. In the morning, someone found some frozen duck eggs outside in a nest from the previous year, and we warmed up inside our parkas and chewed them. Then we packed up, attached the dogs onto their traces and headed west, way out onto the pack ice.'

The land disappeared, he told me, but the wind stayed constant, forcing them to stop frequently to untangle traces and brew a warming cup of tea. Some hunters managed to catch seals that had come to the top of the ice, but their main quarry was walrus. Our dogs, encouraged by the teams next to them, leaned into their harnesses, and they went way out into Baffin Bay, where the ice was thinner due to strong currents.

'I could see the water moving in the leads we crossed,' he said. 'Anyway, hours later, we came to round holes in the thin ice where the walrus had smashed open breathing holes with their heads, and everyone spread out far apart along the leads, harpoons at the ready.'

Danny took up a stance with his harpoon in his right hand and in his left hand the coiled rope, the method demonstrated to him by the other hunters. Here the animal is always harpooned first and then shot. Otherwise, it can sink or escape, so the harpoon rope is belayed by the hunter, a precarious task as there is a danger of being pulled off the ice and under the water by a ton weight walrus. 'None of the walruses came close to me, but two hunters got one each, and everyone, including the dog teams, helped to pull them onto the ice where they were rapidly cut up before freezing solid.'

All hands worked fast on the butchering as a strong wind from the south rose and blew ropes and mitts across the ice. Meat and skin were shared equally among the hunters, including Danny. Feeling the ice begin to move beneath them, they loaded up their harvest onto the *qamutiit* and set off homewards, facing into the blowing snow. Barely able to see the others around them, they had to backtrack to get onto a more solid ice floe before heading toward Northumberland Island to the south. With all the dog teams spread out in the blizzard. Danny stayed vigilant to follow the faint tracks of those ahead in the snow. After an hour of difficult travel, he caught up with another dog team.

'I was very thirsty. We unloaded our *qamutiit*, flipped them on their side with the handlebars touching, and threw a tarp over the top to create a windbreak and shelter so we could boil water for tea.'

Tea breaks are not only good for the hunters, they are also essential for the dogs, who bite the ice out from between their toes so they don't get lame, while the hunter untangles their traces before they get too knotted. Rehydrated, they were on their way again, across more sheets of moving ice and eventually reached the windward side of Northumberland Island with better ice conditions, then continued onwards. The other dog teams appeared out of the void of spindrift as they got closer to the small cabin on the western end of Herbert Island, where they stayed for the night. Benefiting from the shelter of the hills on the island, they reached Inaluk's house in Qeqertassuaq the following day.

After this bedtime story, we both fell into a deep sleep, but in the middle of the night, I was woken by an elderly woman sitting at the bottom of our bed crying.

'Who's that?' I whispered in Danny's ear.

'Naduk's mother,' he whispered, 'she's drunk.'

'I'd better do something to keep her quiet before she wakes the kids.'

I sat up and massaged her back, cooing 'there, there' for a few minutes, and miraculously she calmed down. But then, seconds later, just as I was falling asleep, she resumed a pitiful wailing at the top of her voice, so I tried to comfort her again with soothing gestures. This went on for a long time, and I desperately wanted to sleep. The girls woke up, surprised by the strange apparition at the bottom of the bed. I told them not to worry; Tiki's granny was sad and needed to cry, but she would be fine in the morning. They accepted this explanation, not being slow themselves when it came to howling if things weren't going their way. Exhausted by then, I decided to ignore her lamentation, and she was gone when I woke in the morning.

Alcohol, so freely available for thousands of years in the western world is a recent import for polar people, brought north by southern traders. Unlike southern latitudes, fermentation doesn't naturally occur in this cold part of the world, and its use here has wreaked havoc on many Inuit families. Regulation for controlling its availability is a complex problem, and different approaches have been tried. In the Canadian Arctic, the communities themselves controlled access by either not allowing it in at all (dry communities) or allowing a specified amount with a permit, the result being that bootlegging flourished. In north-west Greenland, an alcohol quota was available every month to each adult, but if one had enough money, the total allowance could be used in one go, or one could even add to it by buying coupons from a non-drinker, leading to a huge monthly binge – which seemed to be happening in the Rasmussen household.

Chapter Eleven

No mention was made of the excessive drinking the following morning. Suulut suggested to Danny that it would be a good idea to swap Little Bitch for one of Talilanguaq's dogs, but he was reluctant to part with her. 'I'll have to think about it,' he told Suulut. Needing some fresh air, we bundled ourselves and the kids in our layers and walked with Danny down to the dogs.

'A good lead dog, like Little Bitch is essential for a team,' he said as we strolled down the slippery hill in the bracing cold air. 'I've put so much work into training her over the winter, teaching her the commands so that the others will follow her. She's really a good lead dog now. I have no idea what kind of dog Talilanguaq will give me. It might be a complete disaster.'

'I know, but you have to take the risk. What choice do we have?' I held Orla's hand and picked my steps on the icy path. 'You said you might have to kill the pups after they were born to dry up her milk so her nipples wouldn't get frostbite, and even then she will not be in good condition and will probably moult and suffer from cold on the long journey.'

He agreed we would swap after the pups were born, and two days later, Little Bitch looked like she was ready to give birth. Danny unchained her from the line on the ice and walked her to a wooden crate lying on its side, outside the back door of Talilanguaq's house. With a roof and sacking for a door, it made a comfy kennel and there she gave birth to four pups. Danny went to see the litter.

'He was totally fearless.' He said, describing Talilanguaq's novel approach to Little Bitch. 'He showed me with growls and whines how dogs are always wary of him at first, then squeal with delight every time they see him. First, he got a stick and put his mitt on it and poked this into the kennel. Then he shoved his face and shoulders straight in behind it. A bold move for someone dealing with a completely strange dog. Little Bitch growled fiercely but didn't bite, and he was able to pat her within a few minutes.'

Two pups died the next day, and Danny was worried the deal might be off. Little Bitch would be unfit for our long return journey back to Grise Fiord.

'I wonder if the walrus hunt was too strenuous and could have caused the pups to die,' he said, gazing out the large front window at the pale blue icebergs moored on the sea ice.

'I don't think so. I remember your friend Ken Mac Rury, saying that a lot of Inuit dog pups die when they're young and that it's natural because only the fittest can survive this tough environment?'

'That's true.'

The other two healthy pups survived, and Talilanguaq was pleased to have new breeding stock from Canada because only two years previously, Qaanaaq lost so many dogs in the distemper outbreak, it greatly reduced the genetic pool. Vaccines were available but had a low uptake among dog owners, I guessed because it's not traditional, and unlike rabies, distemper is not a threat to human health. I was relieved that Little

Bitch and her pups would stay together in their new home. In return, Talilanguaq gave us two dogs: a reddish-brown and white female lead dog called Kaiyoo and another black dog named Kahunga, bringing our team to eleven dogs.

Easter morning, 15 April, the household woke early and Naduk bedecked the living room in yellow – a tablecloth spread on a coffee table covered with serviettes, candles and ornaments. After the Sunday religious service, friends and family arrived for tea, coffee and pastries. In the kitchen, a large frozen halibut was laid out, along with Raymond's frozen muskox from Grise Fiord, all thinly sliced and eaten raw. Alo cut small pieces of the frozen fish and fed Oisín and Orla, who kept asking for more like small open-beaked birds. 'Here,' he said, handing the knife to Danny. 'You father', then he picked up some oily Kiviaq or fermented auks and nibbled with relish, avoiding the feathers.

Naduk left to take part in a football game after the feast, and others went to see the dog sledge races. I followed her, bringing Orla, Oisín and Tempy along to cheer for her team, while Danny needed to do some

Football on the ice.

jobs on the *qamutiik*. At the bottom of the hill, Orla had enough of the abrasive, cold wind and yelled, 'I'm cold!' refusing my bribes to walk back up to the house. A young couple with a small child saw my predicament and offered to pull her along in their little sledge, an invitation she gladly accepted. Later, Danny returned, 'where were you? I couldn't find you at the dog races. Why didn't you come?'

'We had to turn back because Orla was too cold. We didn't see you either.'

'I was down on the ice, lashing my *qamutiik* before going to watch the end of the race. Talilanguaq came second in the fifteen-kilometre dog race, by the way, and another guy from Herbert Island won first place.'

'That's good,' I rescued the Easter candle on the coffee table from Oisín's reach, unwilling to follow Suulut's advice to let him learn from the experience of a burn.

'It's an important event as people here live by their dogs,' Danny continued. 'Anyway … what isn't good is that a hunter I had never met before came up and started talking to me, but I couldn't understand him. So, he drew a map in the snow and indicated that he had just returned from the north, and he seemed to say Smith Sound was all open water. I can't believe this is what he was trying to tell me. It's so early in the season. We walked over to the crowd to find someone who spoke English to interpret, but couldn't find anyone, and after a while, he disappeared. I couldn't find him after that.'

Danny was bothered by this news and, at the same time, inclined to disbelieve it. 'We'll have to find out more about this,' he said. 'I'll find a phone to call Thule Air Base to check if they have any information on the ice conditions further north. They'll have up-to-date charts on the ice.'

Danny told me that Thule Air Base, located about 150 kilometres further south, is a US armed forces installation. It was first established in 1951 during the height of the Cold War. 'The shortest distance from Russia to the US is over the Arctic, so it was built to intercept potential attacks from Russia,' he said. 'An American B-52 bomber crashed on the sea ice near Thule, I think, in 1968; it had nuclear bombs on board that contaminated the area. A clean-up was done quickly, but there are rumours that one of the bombs is still missing.'

I found out later that the air base had been constructed quickly and in secrecy, and that the Inughuit who had established the small village of Uummannaq on this site were never consulted nor given any information or say in what was happening when the Danish government agreed to the American air base. Two years later, in 1953, they were told they would have to vacate their homes and move to another area further north. Given less than a week to leave, twenty-seven families packed all their belongings into sledges to move to different places areas. Thirteen families took the arduous journey to Qaanaaq through a glacier and on the sea ice. When they arrived, they found a few inadequate tents, the materials for their promised wooden huts didn't come until months later at the end of summer. Like the relocation to Grise Fiord, this whole episode deeply affected the people of Qaanaaq. With little or no information given to them, suspicion, distrust and fear about what goes on at Thule, as well as the possible negative effects on their environment, livelihood and culture, were rife. A high-tech nuclear missile defence system right beside peaceful, isolated people who have no say in the political forces that affect them was another injustice added to my growing awareness of the effects of colonisation in the Arctic.

The next day, still in disbelief, Danny phoned the base from the municipal office. He was informed that regular ice reconnaissance flights were conducted over Smith Sound and that one was scheduled for the following day. When he called back the next day, they confirmed that all the ice had indeed shifted out of Smith Sound and into Kane Basin, leaving open water as far north as 79 degrees. This was farther north than where we had planned the sea crossing, but Danny was determined to find a way to do it. He called Borak Air, the company in Resolute Bay we had used to charter the flight to Greenland, to see if they could fly us to Alexander Fiord on the east coast of Ellesmere Island, but they were noncommittal and wouldn't know for a week. It looked bleak.

And so was the weather. Over the next few days, heavy snow fell with a driving wind, and I began to feel trapped. Suulut and Naduk were drinking, and their children would either go stay at a friend's house or lock themselves in their bedrooms. On one such evening, Suulut brought Blackie, his lead dog, into the house. When Danny pointed out that Blackie was peeing on the floor, Suulut responded, 'that's okay, he can do what he wants.' And like a wayward child, Blackie seized his opportunity, stood up at the table, and ate the food off the plates, then wandered out of the house to roam the town. Suulut fell asleep in a chair, then Tiki woke him up and successfully coaxed him to go to bed.

While all this was going on, I distracted myself by reading about Qitdlarssuaqs journey. Having met the Greenland hunters, the migrants went with them to their camp at Pitoravik, north-west of Qaanaaq, and found the rest of the group living in dreadful, impoverished conditions. Many years before, an epidemic had killed the old people and their kayak and bows and arrows had been buried with them according to tradition. The young men no longer knew how to make these things and, therefore, could not hunt marine mammals during the summer. They also could not catch the abundant fish in the lakes or hunt the caribou. Their diet was restricted to walrus, polar bears, seals and auks in the summer. The Baffin Island Inuit re-introduced the kayak for summer hunting on the sea and bows and arrows for hunting caribou on land, as well as the *kakivak* or three-pronged spear for fishing. They also taught them how to build the stronger spiral domed *iglu* with a long entrance passage at a lower level to retain heat, all of which made a vast improvement to the lives of the Inughuit in this part of Greenland.

The Canadian Inuit stayed for seven years, then Qitdlarssuaq, now older and unwell, yearned to see his homeland again. He set off with his followers, though unsurprisingly, Ivalu with her family and a few others opted to stay, which was a good decision because the travellers never made it back to Baffin Island. Qitdlarssuaq died early in the trip on Ellesmere Island at *Qitdlaqarvik* (the place where Qitllaq lies) near Cape Herschel, and without their leader, the rest of the group wandered, suffering starvation, famine, murder and even cannibalism at *Perdlerarvigssuaq* (the place of the great famine) in Makinson Inlet. Nowadays, many people from Grise Fiord believe this place is haunted, though it doesn't stop them from camping there to fish. Of the twenty healthy people who left Greenland, only a small, ragged group of three adults and two children survived. They decided to return to Greenland, arriving the following spring, where they settled and passed on their amazing story of human endurance and courage to future generations. I closed the book and checked on Oisín, who had woken from his afternoon nap. He was quietly playing with one of Tiki's toy cars. Still thinking about Qitdlarssuaq, it occurred to me that the Inughuit of Qaanaaq have now preserved their old ways of hunting, much better than the Canadian Inuit. Skidoos were banned here because it was thought the engine noise scares the seals away. There were only two skidoos here, one owned by the police and the other by the Royal Danish Trading Company. I suspected it was just a matter of time before many traditions would be lost again with the pervasive influence of modern life.

The 19 April was Angu's sixteenth birthday. Again, the low table in the living room was laid out with coffee and pastries early in the morning. Suulut gave Angu his stereo as a birthday present and set it up for him in his bedroom. A topless girl calendar from the previous year lay scrunched in the rubbish bin. At sixteen, Suulut proudly said, 'Angu is a man now and can have real girls in his bedroom'. Angu, tall and handsome, sat on his bed with his cousin Gertee, and blew up some Durex, which they were idly playing with.

Around midday, when the sun was high, Angu took Tiki, Gertee, Orla, and Tempy out, along with the Durex balloons, to play in the snow. Danny and I went with Oisín to check on the dogs; we met Suulut *en route*, carrying a case of beer back to the house, so we took our time. On our return, he had finished most of the beer, and Naduk was drinking spirits. The boys brought our kids back and then disappeared for the rest of the day, an ominous sign. I kept out of the way, entertaining the children, and wondered about the cause of the alcohol problem for many circumpolar people. I presumed the traumatic impact of colonisation, with the effects of disempowerment and upheavals in their way of life, was a big contributor to this.

We had planned to go to Herbert Island to camp there for a few days, but Tempy started vomiting due to gastroenteritis, and I felt I was coming down with a viral illness as well, so we had to postpone that trip. We decided, no matter what, to move out and camp on the ice below the town the following morning. It was time to acclimatise to living in the cold outdoors, which now seemed like a very appealing prospect. At the same time, being careful not to offend Suulut and his family, who never asked for anything in return for their kindness, we highlighted our need to move on to the ice to prepare for our journey back to Grise Fiord.

Chapter Twelve

A flat area behind a group of substantial ice hummocks hid our small camp on the ice below the town from view of the seaward-facing houses. Exposed with no warm house for shelter, the cold was inescapable, but we needed to get used to our tent home. With little to amuse them, the kids became bored and cantankerous. I occupied them with our one game of Snakes and Ladders, and when they tired of that, Danny hitched up the dogs and we set off on a trip to Herbert Island. It was 8.30 p.m. but we didn't need to worry about darkness, the sun was low in the sky, dipping further to the horizon towards midnight, creating one long dusk before rising again. The ever-present wind strengthened, dropping the temperature even further. In the lee of a lofty pinnacled iceberg, we met Talilanguaq and Savfaq heading back to Qaanaaq and stopped to chat. With animated gestures, they informed us they would accompany us on the first part of our journey back to Canada, the sea ice crossing, to guide us through the formidable pressure ice on the north end of Kane Basin. Savfaq mimed how she would help me with the children and Talilanguaq insisted that this was a good idea. They were both knowledgeable and experienced travellers in this area where they have hunted polar bears for years, but Danny was unsure it would work for us. It would take us very far north from our route and then we would have to swing back to the south again and possibly encounter more broken pack ice and open water, meanwhile depleting our precious supplies. We were non-committal, and no provisional date was mentioned, hunters only go when the conditions are right.

Tempy, was still not feeling well after her bout of gastroenteritis, and Orla said she was sick too, although she looked healthy. After an hour of travel, we rounded a huge wedge-shaped iceberg, calved from one of the many nearby glaciers, and turned back for our little camp home on the ice. The tent warmed up once we got the stove going and

The girls amuse themselves on the ice below Qaanaaq.

Oisín plays in the box on the qamutiik.

the children wrapped in their sleeping bags, but toileting outside on the sea ice was challenging, especially for Orla. Tempy mastered it without difficulty, but Orla could not perform, she tensed her muscles when her bare bottom was exposed to the frigid elements. Like Oisín, she would have to wear nappies again. Danny had another idea, he bought a plastic bucket and made a cardboard toilet seat for use at night in the tent, it was kept outside conveniently by the entrance and this solution worked well. Morning brought a heavy, overcast sky but at least the wind had died down. We set off again for Herbert Island. Getting the dogs and the *qamutiik* ready occupied us, and it was good to keep integrating our two new dogs into the team. Kaiyoo, our new lead dog, settled in well. Danny changed his commands to the Greenland version of 'right' and 'left', which she understood and obeyed, and the rest of the dogs followed her.

Before we attached all the dogs to the *qamutiik*, Tempy and Orla were tucked into the box with sleeping bags around them, while Oisín preferred being in my *amauti*. Once the dogs' traces were secured to the *qamutiik*, Danny and I jumped on the front as it shot off towards Herbert Island. I wanted to see the place where the British explorer Wally Herbert had brought his wife Marie and ten-month-old daughter, Kari, to spend

Qamutiik *travelling on the sea ice.*

two years living with the Polar Eskimos, as the Inughuit of this area were called at that time. Marie wrote a book about her time here, called *The Snow People,* where she describes her initial shock on arrival by boat at the end of the summer of 1971. The cold bleakness of the barren rock island that would be her home left her speechless in dismay. At least I was not alone in having doubts about my partner's polar travel plans. Marie settled in so well to life in the tiny community that they stayed for over a year, despite the hardships of living in a small hut with no facilities such as a bathroom or running water. Herbert Island was not named after this family, but coincidently another Herbert, a crew member with the Inglefield expedition who explored this area in the 1840s.

The Scottish mountaineer and author, Myrtle Simpson also brought her young children with her on her expeditions. In 1969, she made a valiant but unsuccessful attempt to reach the North Pole from Ward Hunt Island off Northern Ellesmere with her husband Hugh and their friend Roger. Her three children, the eldest aged eight at that time, stayed in Resolute Bay, the next community south of Grise Fiord, with a childminder they brought with them from Scotland while the parents made their North Pole attempt in extremely difficult conditions. After they returned to Resolute Bay, the whole family then spent weeks in the summer camped on Cape Sparbo on Devon Island, living in a tent and enjoying the freedom of the open landscape. In her book about this journey, *Due North*, she explains that it never occurred to her to leave her children behind; they came with her on all her travels through the jungles of Guyana, and the glaciers of Greenland.

Sitting on a box that was tied to the front of the *qamutiik* and thinking about these inspirational women as the runners glided over the smooth snow eased my anxieties about the long journey back to Grise Fiord. Although I did note that when they were going on long Arctic journeys, they left their children in the safety of an Inuit village.

For now, the ice was flat and polished, with no cracks, and after a while, the dogs tired of their initial enthusiastic pace and settled into a slower, rhythmic, pulling trot – a hypnotic speed that lulled the children to sleep. It had the same effect on me, but I had to resist the urge to close my eyes, or I would fall off my perch. Closer to Herbert Island, they gathered speed again. We stopped them just before the tide crack and tied them out by fixing the long chain to the sea ice. Gathering the children, Danny introduced me to Inaluk, who he had met when going on the walrus hunt. She invited us back to her house for a cup of tea and brought us around the tiny community of 'Qeqertassuaq', with its many empty houses. The gloomy, grey, overcast light magnified the subdued atmosphere. Today, it is deserted, being used only occasionally by hunters.

On the way back to Qaanaaq, Danny told me that three years before, Inaluk was out hunting polar bears in the Kane Basin area with her husband when he developed severe abdominal pain, apparently from appendicitis and died before the rescue helicopter finally arrived from Qaanaaq – a reminder that not all hazards are thin ice and open water.

'What a tragic thing to happen, way out there beyond rescue, although it's very unlikely to happen to us. My main concern, as I keep telling you, is that the journey will be too hard on the children. It goes against my maternal instinct to provide them with comfort and safety.'

Our tent in Qaanaaq.

'They'll be fine, look at them, tucked up and cosy in their little nest.'

The prospect of open water made me uneasy, especially having heard about the ice conditions on Smith Sound. Talilanguaq thought crossing further north at the top of Kane Basin might be possible, but this would not be a smooth crossing. Enormous ridges of ice stack up due to the action of sea currents in this area which makes for difficult travel, and although he was keen to come with us to show us the best crossing, I had a feeling this arrangement might not materialise.

'I don't think we can rely on Talilanguaq to come despite what he says and we're probably better to go ourselves.' Danny said. 'He might want to guide us for a fee and then do polar bear hunting on the side, but we don't have the money for that.' 'Okay, but if I think it's too dangerous, we have to turn back.'

'Of course.' He thought I was fussing. The children had warm clothes, plenty of food, and shelter in the tent; they would be fine. Don't forget, if we are delayed, there are emergency rations stored in an old RCMP cabin at Alexandra Fiord, and we also have the radio. So, if we get into difficulty, we can call our friends in Grise Fiord for assistance if we really need to. It's unfortunate that they don't use single sideband radios here, though. The following day, back at our tent, we got lots of visitors, all at the same time, curious about our camp and wanting to know more about our plans. Danny invited everyone into the tent for tea. First, four hunters crammed into our small space. 'Come in, come in', Danny beckoned to more people outside. I couldn't believe five more bodies squeezed through the entrance; we were on top of each other. In a spasm of claustrophobia, I bailed out with the children. Snow began to fall and the temperature felt like a pleasant -20. The girls climbed ice hummocks and played a short game of hide and seek around them. Our visitors didn't stay long. After the tea, they examined some of Danny's Canadian Inuit-style dog sledding equipment. One man shook his head, saying, 'no good, no good'. Danny laughed it off but later admitted it irked him a bit, 'Anything a bit different to the local gear, they always say no good, just because it's not the traditional Greenland gear that they are used to, even when it is traditional Grise Fiord gear. The design of almost everything they use goes back hundreds of years, and they stick to it.'

The season advanced, and the first day of May arrived, our day of departure, but we had not heard from Talilanguaq or Savfaq, and we could not wait for them. Everything we needed for the trip was ready. We had been waiting for the weather to cooperate, and although we woke to another overcast day with limited visibility, we packed the qamutiik and lashed it down, determined to make a start and cover a few kilometres of the journey. As soon as we set off, snow fell and after an initial burst of energy the dogs slowed down to a sedate pace. The accumulation of soft, sticky snow combined with the heavy load on the qamutiik made pulling harder. After a few hours, the girls started quarrelling, they were tired of being cooped up in their small shelter on the qamutiik. We made stops for snacks and stretching of legs, as well as nappy changes which

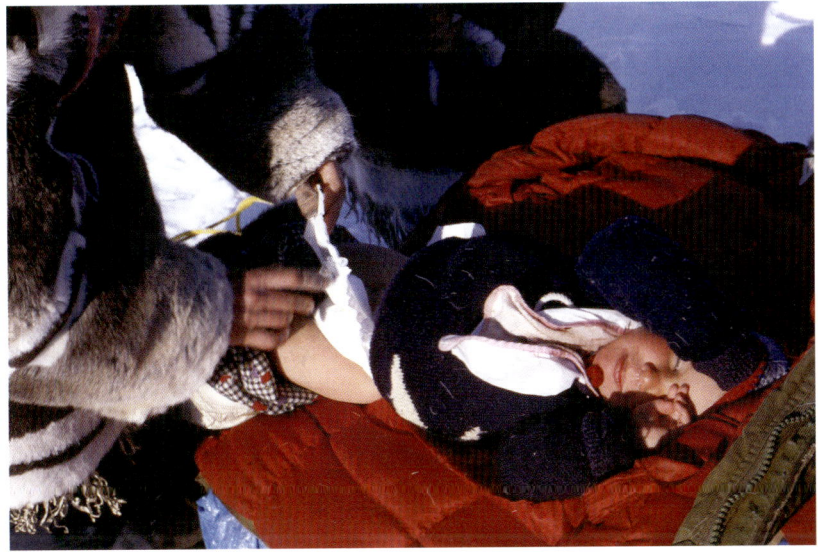

Nappy change on the **qamutiik.** *Our fur clothes shed hairs everywhere, especially on our food.*

had to be done at great speed on the qamutiik , but then the wind strengthened, blowing the snow around us, into our faces, and down our sleeves, forcing these stops to be brief.

Pressing on to cover more kilometres, the girls gave up complaining and fell asleep. As the weather closed in on us even more and I ruminated on a foreboding as heavy as the dull, leaden sky above me. After eight hours on the move, we needed to find a suitable place to camp. Following the coast northwards, we continuously scanned the area for a sheltered spot and an hour later, Danny pointed towards the shore, to a small brown square barely visible in the driving snow. 'Look Ger! I think that could be a hunter's cabin. We should go in that direction and check it out.'

'Yes. I hope it is.'

Despite our exhaustion, we veered to the right with renewed energy and pushed against the wind, which had grown stronger, whipping the snow against us. With the discovery of the cabin there was no need to spend time erecting our tent, the small, empty wooden shelter with two sleeping platforms, was a luxury. We unloaded our gear and threw the bags inside. I sorted the children while Danny looked after the dogs. He searched outside for a place to secure their chain on the hard windswept icy ground, but it wasn't easy. I saw him struggling to find anywhere suitable in the blizzard, and realising this job was going to take longer than expected, he came in for a cup of warm tea while all the dogs lay down after their strenuous day's work.

'Why don't you use the Greenland method of tying out the dogs from one anchor?' I suggested, raising dust as I vigorously swept the floor with a broom I had discovered.

'No. I haven't done it with them before. They could fight.'

'They know each other very well by now,' I persisted. 'It'll be so much easier and quicker. It'll take you at least an hour or more to find a good place, attach that long chain, and then tie each dog to it. Why not try the Greenland way?'

'It's risky.' He gazed out the front window towards the peacefully resting dogs.

Inside the hunter's cabin, Tempy finds a comic.

'Well try it out now. Tie them close to the window so we can keep an eye on them, and if there's a problem, we can sort it out.'

Still not convinced, he agreed to try it, and in a short time, all the dogs were staked out in two bunches close to the cabin. After being fed, they lay down quietly. Meanwhile, I spread out our sleeping bags on the sleeping platform and the children were happy to help me make this 'house' comfortable. With our cooking stove lit, the whole cabin warmed, and after a meal of steaming freeze-dried beef stew, biscuits and hot chocolate, sleep was irresistible. We turned off the stove and made a last check on the dogs, who were curled up, nose to tail, blanketed by the falling snow. Tempy and Orla were lively after their nap on the journey, but with the stove off, there was no danger if their parents slept while they investigated the contents of the bags and played together.

I drifted off to a deep slumber, and after some time, loud growls and snarls of savage dogs seeped into my dreams. Rousing myself I registered in horror it wasn't a dream, it was our own dogs outside.

'Danny,' I shook him. 'The dogs are fighting'

He shot out of his sleeping bag and grabbed the whip, I followed him, throwing on my boots and parka over thermal underwear.

Outside an appalling sight of dogs in a tangled ball of vicious growling, biting, blood-stained fur assailed us, their traces tightly intertwined, so every dog was ferociously biting the dog beside him. Danny lashed his whip to subdue the brawl. Eventually, they calmed enough for us to start untangling. As we began separating them, we could see a dog in the middle was seriously injured. Johnny, his white fur now pink, lay very still at the bottom of the heap. Danny unclipped him from the bunch. 'This looks very bad; we'll have to bring him inside.'

I opened the door as he carried him in and laid him on the floor. The children were now awake and wide-eyed, sitting up on the sleeping platform. We all watched in dazed silence. Johnny didn't move, then he twitched, convulsed, vomited and died. Tempy was stunned, 'what's wrong with him, is he sick?' I explained the fight to her, and that Johnny had died. She thought about it. It was a lot to take in, for all of us. Her siblings were too young to comprehend it and soon started squabbling and wanting food.

Danny brought the body outside to bury under stones and tied the rest of the dogs out on the long chain. I cleaned up the mess on the floor, feeling very guilty. If I had not insisted that the dogs be staked in that way, this would not have happened. We only had eleven dogs now, which was still enough power for the *qamutiik*, but losing one so early felt like a bad omen. I continued to berate myself as I cooked the porridge and boiled the kettle for tea.

'None of them are injured badly or need stitches,' he said coming in after checking each dog. 'They're tough as old boots.'

After breakfast, I couldn't wait to leave this gloomy place. When Johnny was buried, we packed up and were off again, the children content with full stomachs and plenty of sleep. The sky cleared, while the sea ice, polished by the previous day's wind, was smooth and fast for the dogs, allowing us to make good mileage. My mood lightened as we continued travelling north-west. Sitting on the *qamutiik*, swaying gently with its soothing motion, and watching to my right, the rise and fall of the coastline with rocky outcrops pushing through the covering of snow, all my apprehensions and guilt dissipated. To my left, on the other side, the expanse of sea ice seemed boundless, timeless, untouched. Only the rhythmic swish of the runners broke the silence of this raw, primal landscape. Our dog footprints and those of the runners are the only marks on the flawless snow. We travelled onwards, the children slept, and time passed in this tranquil state. When they woke, it was time for a hot drink and snack break, with rapid nappy changes and a quick run in the snow. Baring bottoms to the elements was getting easier when there was no wind, even in temperatures in the -20ºs. Pressing ahead, we didn't go into the fiord to visit Siorapaluk, the last outpost camp on the coast, but continued westward, making good progress.

Towards evening, the weather deteriorated, snow fell, and visibility was reduced to 100 metres ahead. The dogs were tiring, slowed again by the soft snow, but we had to keep going while we could. When we

We meet Greenland hunters who give us bad news.

got closer to a promontory, a group of dog teams emerged in the murky distance. We stopped as they approached, and Danny went over to speak to them. I stayed with our *qamutiik*, brandishing the whip in front of our dogs to make sure there was no opportunity for advancing to fight with the other teams, all the while admiring the hunters clad in their splendid polar bear skin pants. With a combination of gestures and the occasional word in English, they told Danny there was no way of crossing over the sea ice to Canada. One of the hunters drew a map in the snow with his whip, showing where the ice had already broken up. Even their polar bear hunting excursion had to be curtailed due to the early breakup, all they could get were a few seals. Danny was devastated by this news.

'Maybe we should continue and check if there might be a route,' he said after the hunters went off towards Qaanaaq. He still held on to the hope that there would be an ice bridge further north.

'No. I don't think that's a good idea, we could find ourselves in trouble on shifting ice and open water.' It seemed pointless to me, given the information from the Thule Air Base, other Inughuit who had been north, and now this group of hunters all agreeing that this was an unusual year for the ice to move out so soon.

'Hmm. Let's have a brew up and think about what to do now,' he said.

'You know it's a good thing we met those hunters,' I reflected, unpacking our stove and cups. 'It's better to know now that we can't get across than getting stuck halfway over.'

'I think we should go back to Qaanaaq and see if we can get more information on the condition of the ice. This is far too early for the ice to go out. It's never broken up this early before.'

'I wonder if it's due to global warming. I read an article about that somewhere. Apparently, the earth heating due to greenhouse gases.' At this time, the concept of climate change was barely recognised by the general public, but the media was beginning to take an interest in reports from scientists such as James Hansen, who outlined human-induced climate change to a US Senate committee in 1988, and the International Panel on Climate Change was set up that year. There were also plenty of deniers to confuse the picture.

'I don't know, it could just be a warmer year.' Danny said, looking into the distance, only half listening to me as he tried to figure out how to get across this open water. So much physical, mental and emotional effort went into planning this journey that Danny needed to be utterly convinced it was impossible to do. He loved the challenge of an ambitious goal and exploring rarely visited polar landscapes.

'You know, now that I think about it,' I said, rummaging through Ziploc bags to find the tea bags 'when I asked Ooleesie about the biggest change in her life today compared to when she was young, she told me it rains in the summer now and it only snowed when she was young, never rain. I expected she would mention some cultural change, but now it makes sense if the climate is getting warmer. Anyway, we can still do journeys with the dogs. There are other places to explore here.' I was beginning to see the silver lining in our dilemma, and I didn't have the same need to make an epic journey, when shorter trips were just as exciting and full of wonder in this environment.

In the end, climate change had decided for us, although at that time we didn't understand its scale or that these were signs of the biggest threat to humanity in the world today. Years later, looking at a graph of sea ice extent in the Arctic, we saw that the spring of 1990 had the lowest sea ice level on record at that time, and since then it has dramatically reduced even further, both in extent and thickness. Today we could not even consider making our intended journey, and in the next decade summer sea ice in the Arctic Ocean may disappear completely, exposing dark water that doesn't reflect sunlight and heat back into the atmosphere. The consequences of these changes affect not only the people and animals who live in this cold region of our planet but everyone because polar sea ice influences temperatures and sea levels in other parts of the world too.

Chapter Thirteen

Back in Qaanaaq, we camped again on the ice below the town and Danny went to speak to Talilanguaq and other hunters who knew the area well. There was unanimity that Smith Sound had open water way up into Kane Basin, and none of the elders remembered that ever happening so early in the season. Our only option was to fly back to Grise Fiord, even though we had no budget for this additional charter, but we would have to figure that out later. Danny rang Kenn Borak Air, who told him they would be busy for the next week, or longer, supplying flights for the Canadian Government's Polar Continental Shelf Program, which provides logistical services to scientific researchers. After that, it might be possible, weather permitting. The next morning, we called over to Suulut, who was outside his house repairing his qamutiik in the spring sunshine. With Danny helping him lash on the napooks (crosspieces), he told us he was going on an ice fishing trip to Bowdoin Fiord, and he asked us to join him. Hastily, we retreated to our camp, packed all our belongings, including our tent since we planned to stay overnight, and secured everything onto the qamutiik. When Suulut got his dogs ready, we hitched our team onto our qamutiik too, and followed him across the ice, around a headland, turning south, where a wall of spectacularly high red vertical cliffs towered above us as we sped over the smooth sea ice, our dogs eager to catch up with the team ahead despite the heavier load.

After a couple of hours, we stopped for tea and Danny used the opportunity to untangle the traces, which needed to be done regularly with dogs changing positions and plaiting the ropes into an icy sinewy tree trunk from which the shortened leads branched. This task usually necessitated using bare fingers, risking frostbite in the depths of winter, but Akeeagok had shown Danny how to do it in a way that allowed the use of mitts. Making good speed, we turned into a narrow fiord sheltered from the wind, and a few kilometres later, Suulut pointed to a small wooden cabin nestled under low hills, an empty meat rack stood near the shore. He told us that it once belonged to Navarana, the Inuit wife of the Danish explorer and author Peter Freuchen. Navarana was the granddaughter of Merqusaq, who as a young man, was part Qitdlarssauq's

Danny untangles the traces.

The small cabin that once belonged to Navarana.

Tempy was fascinated by the low door.

Making ourselves at home in the cabin.

migratory group. Fruechen, spent many years living with the people of this area since the early 1900s and recounted stories old Merqusaq told him. He gave a harrowing account of their attempted return journey to Canada in his *Book of the Eskimos*. When I first read about it, it sounded brutal, but it's hard for us to imagine today how incredibly tough life was for the Inuit at that time, starvation always shadowed them as they moved about in search of game.

We went straight to the cabin, now only used by hunters it was basic but adequate. Tempy was fascinated by the heat conserving door, which just about reached the top of her head. I was more interested in a small potbellied stove while Orla and Oisín sat, mute and unsure of the dark gloom inside in contrast to the brilliant light outdoors. I found a broom and, after a small clean-up, decided housekeeping, unpacking and making ourselves at home would have to wait; there were fish to be caught. Freuchen wrote about the rarity of fish in the diet of the people of this area back in 1911. According to him, no self-respecting hunter would fish for something that volunteered to be caught, and only occasionally,

Suulut and his dog team on the way to Bowdoin Fiord.

in the summer, an old woman might catch a few. I'm not sure that was true; he was prone to exaggeration, and fortunately, those attitudes no longer existed. Fishing in Greenland today is their most important industry, using trawlers to haul up thousands of tons of halibut annually.

We followed Suulut and Danny, who had gone down to the sea ice to find the right spot for fishing; it had to be over an undersea valley as the Greenland halibut are bottom fish found in deep waters. The surrounding headlands and other rocky landmarks helped with orientation, and Suulut and Danny made a hole in the ice using an auger or handheld ice fishing drill about thirty centimetres in diameter. It didn't take long to get through to water, the sea ice being less thick here than on the Canadian side due to a warm current that comes up the west coast of Greenland. A long line of baited hooks, coiled and stuck into the sides of a cardboard box, was ready to be attached to the metre-long glider; a wooden plank with a fin and a metal nose. Having worked out the line of the undersea valley, Suulut then launched the glider through the hole in the right direction, where it dragged the cord of baited hooks under the ice as we fed them out. Cleaning the snow from the surface of the ice, we could see the glider moving underneath, so Danny and Suulut cut another hole, about ten metres from the first, and brought the glider up. They attached a lump of metal with an eyelet to the fishing line, secured the line at the surface, and dropped the metal down the hole to bring the line to the bottom of the fiord. A similar weight was fixed to the line at the first hole, so now all the baited hooks lay on the seabed.

Back in the cabin, waiting for the fish to bite, Danny inspected the potbellied stove. Having removed the top and looked up the chimney, he said it was falling apart and could not be used, so he installed our camping stove on top of it instead, pumping the naphtha bottle to get the two burners going.

'This will keep the place warm. I'm going to see to the dogs now,' he said, bending down to go out the low door, 'and Suulut said he would come up in a while for tea.'

Tempy was intrigued by the cabin. 'Did small people once live here?' she wanted to know as she helped me find cups and tea in the food box.

'Are we going to sleep here tonight?' she asked.

'Yes. Would you prefer to sleep in the tent?'

'No. I want to sleep here. But not beside Orla.'

After a snack of instant soup, cheese and crackers, we went out to look around. Tempy found a small slope to slide on and Orla followed her, then it was time to see if we had any fish. We stood

*Suulut pulls out fish.
... and more fish.*

around the hole in the ice, watching Suulut and Danny pull up a length of the line. Like conjurers performing a magical trick, a grey flat fish emerged about 35 centimetres long, attached to a hook, and then another and more as the line was pulled out. They unhooked them and threw them on the snow, where we got a closer look.

The bottom side of their body was paler than the top and had no eyes; it had migrated to the dorsal ridge of the head, and the mouth was full of sharp teeth, making it look quite fierce. When all the line was pulled out, we helped coil it back inside the cardboard box, attaching the sixty hooks carefully to the side. The wind was rising, and Suulut was eager to return to Qaanaaq. With a catch of more than twenty halibut of all sizes, we accepted one for our dinner. He put the rest in his fish box to take back and sell to the fish processing plant. Unlike the Canadian Inuit, who share their catch, the Greenlanders are willing to buy and sell their fish, walrus, seal and other traditional food. We fried our fish for dinner and then got into our sleeping bags. During the night, I listened to the wind flinging snow against the windows, snug in the warm cabin.

The next day was silent and bright. The wind had completely slackened, and beneath a clear blue sky, the sun cast shadows on the fluted cliff face across the fiord, folding them into pleats. Nothing stirred, not even the dogs dozing on the ice below us. At last, it was a perfect Arctic spring day.

'I remember a piece that Peter Freuchen wrote about Navarana,' I said to Danny as we began packing up after breakfast. 'She wanted to know what life was like for women in Denmark, and when he explained their usual domestic role, she felt sorry for them. This was, of course, about seventy years ago. Anyway, she couldn't imagine living there without difficult and dangerous journeys and no opportunity to test what you can achieve.'

'You're having lots of opportunities to test that,' he laughed, grabbing some packs to bring down to the *qamutiik*. As we loaded up, the children played, sliding in the sunshine without their heavy parkas on, while the dogs watched us with ears pricked, about a hundred metres from the *qamutiik*.

The children played sliding in the sunshine.

'We have to walk the dogs over to the *qamutiik*,' he said. 'If you take them, I'll walk in front with the whip'.

'Do you mean all ten at one go?'

'Yes. It will take too long to do it individually.'

'Okay …' I paused. 'It won't work, they'll run off and pull me along.'

'They won't, the whip will keep them under control.'

With trepidation, I held the dogs, while Danny walked in front of them flicking the whip from side to side to stop them running past him.

Like an electric current travelling up the leads, their powerful, barely suppressed energy was riveting and unnerving, they could at any moment bolt for freedom.

'I can feel their immense strength. If they take off, I'm letting go,' I warned him, but we got to the *qamutiik* without incident, and we were off again skimming over the sea ice until the dogs expended their usual starting line exuberance. Because it was such a magnificent day, we decided to explore more of Bowdoin fiord, named after Robert Peary's ship, before

Tempy goes out to chop ice.

Tea break on our travels.

heading back to Qaanaaq. Not a cloud in the sky, the snow dazzled, the whole vista ethereal as if we were travelling on top of the clouds.

Lost in my own thoughts, I tried to imagine what it must have been like for Peary's wife Josephine to come here with her husband at eight months pregnant with their first baby in 1893. Their daughter, Marie Ahnighito, was born in a cabin on this fiord. It was unusual for a western woman at that time to accompany her husband on Arctic journeys and, especially, to risk a birth in such a remote place, but she had only been married four years, and most of this time, he was in the Arctic preparing for his attempt at reaching the North Pole.

At least she had some idea of what to expect, she had travelled with him on his second expedition in 1891–92 and had over-wintered then. Her third trip North, six years later, was intended as a surprise visit to him, but it was Josephine who had the surprise. Travelling with her young daughter on a relief ship, they became stuck in the ice near Pim Island off Ellesmere Island while her husband, at the time, was much further north at Fort Conger. While she waited in the ice-bound vessel, a young Inuit woman came on board with a baby in her *amauti* who she introduced as Robert Peary's son. Many polar explorers had sexual partners while in the Arctic, and usually, their wives never found out. Although she was deeply wounded, especially as she was still grieving the death of her second baby who had been born six months after her husband left for the Arctic, Josephine kept this secret and continued to support her his polar achievements all her life. The Inuit children of Peary, Henson and other explorers were accepted as equals in Inuit society, but it wasn't the same down south. It took until two years before we arrived north for a 'North Pole Family Reunion' to take place with the American side of the families.

My reveries were suddenly interrupted. Both Danny and I, sitting at the front of the *qamutiik*, simultaneously saw the dogs running straight towards a large ice chunk protruding from a tide crack. We both jumped off just seconds before the qamutiik rose up onto it and turned over, spilling the contents of the box, including the children, onto the soft snow.

'Why did you do that?' Tempy wailed, although unhurt.

'I didn't do anything. The dogs went over the ice themselves.' I tried not to laugh.

'You did because you and Dad got off.' She continued sobbing, and Orla joined in.

'You're all right. You didn't get hurt,' I stroked her back.

'Where's Oisín?' Danny searched the upturned box as I surveyed the scattered items on the snow. No sign of a baby.

'Here he is!' I lifted a sleeping bag on the ice – and there he lay, emerging from a deep sleep totally undisturbed by the crash, cushioned and cocooned in our sleeping bags. We laughed at dozy Oisín, and the girls' tears dried up.

Farther out, cruising along the fiord, Danny noticed a small object lying on the ice and picked up the white cardboard lid of a fancy chocolate box, decorated with a red satin ribbon. Tempy immediately claimed it, turning it over, elated to find inside a menu of the contents illustrated in gold. 'Madam, what would you like?' she inquired, proffering the lid to me to select a chocolate delicacy. I played along with her, and despite being a chocoholic, the lavish concoctions were so unobtainable I had no cravings. Hours of fun passed with this treasured piece of cardboard, including conjectures of how it had landed on the ice in the middle of nowhere, keeping everyone occupied on the way back to Qaanaaq. Finding the chocolate box lid reminded me of an episode in the Qitdlarssuaq story. One time, when they travelled along the coast, they saw a giant with long hair in the distance on the shore. Terrified as the dogs galloped towards it, Qitdlarssuaq, drawing on his shamanic powers shouted 'whalebone, whalebone'. The giant became smaller as they got closer, and when they arrived at the shore, they saw only a whale's jawbone sticking up out of the snow. Another time, while travelling on the pack ice, they saw a crowd of naked people in front of them, and as the dogs raced ahead, Qitdlarssuaq shouted, 'algae, algae', and suddenly the creatures were algae.

Orla's thick caribou parka did not allow her to bend her elbow enough to feed herself.

Sometimes local children came to play with our kids.

My rational brain could relate to how easily shapes can transform up here, too, with limitless vistas in the intense light and varying shades of blue and white. Optical illusions such as mirages are not unusual in the Arctic when the air starts to heat up in the spring, bending the light over the cooler ice and reflecting images in the air. Pink snow can be seen too in tidal ice, due to a particular cryophilic alga. The British explorer, Captain John Ross, searching for the Northwest Passage in 1818, described crimson snow streaking the cliffs of Northwest Greenland like rivers of blood.

On our return, we checked the status of our flight to Grise Fiord. Rising temperatures were bringing low clouds, flurries of snow and poor visibility. Not the weather for landing a plane, and the pilots had to have a good forecast for both the Qaanaaq and Grise Fiord landings before they would attempt the journey. We had to sit tight in our little tent on the ice and wait until there was a window in the weather. No more trips out to fishing camps, we needed to be ready to go as soon as the plane left Resolute Bay. Endless games of Snakes and Ladders were played in the tent, or visits to watch movies such as the first Batman movie on Suulut's television. Sometimes, local children came to play with our kids, it didn't matter that they didn't speak the same language, and with the weather warming, we shed our carapace of heavy skin parkas to enjoy the freedom of easy movement for a short period around midday. Orla's thick, stiff caribou parka did not allow her to bend her elbow enough to feed herself. She yelled in frustration at being thwarted when she tried to bring a spoonful of food to her mouth. Much to her sister's amusement, I had to spoon-feed her like a baby.

When the sun dipped in the evening, the deep Arctic silence was punctured by howls from a dog team in the distance.

'Shhh … girls, listen to the dogs singing for their supper,' I said, disturbing their snow-digging game as the howls were taken up by neighbouring teams and spread to farther teams until all the dogs of the

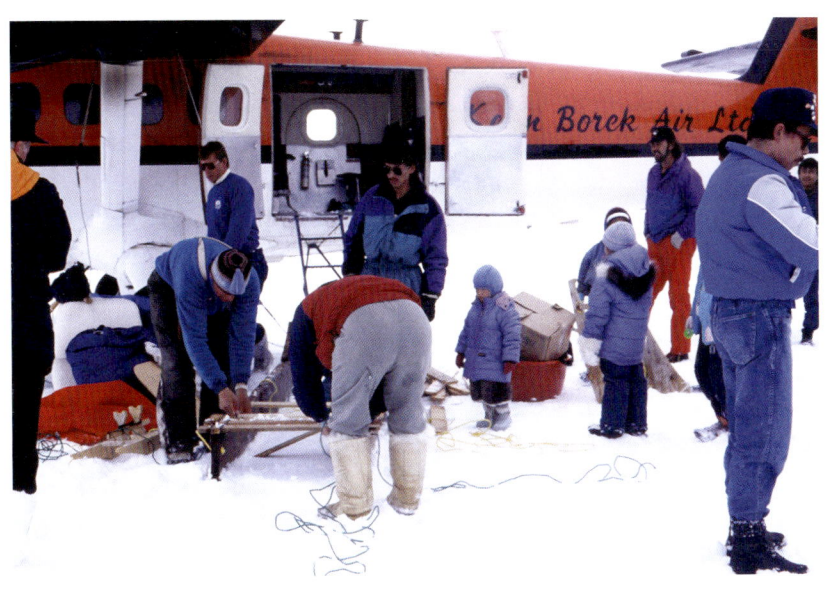

Packing our gear into the plane. Suulut helps Danny.

The co-pilot stretched over the fuel barrels to refuel.

town were howling in harmony. A slow a cappella with slightly ominous overtones it swelled and built to a crescendo and then faded. With more dogs than people in the town, they were making their presence felt.

Finally, after a week of waiting, the weather report was good and the Twin Otter landed on the sea ice. In a flurry of activity, we hitched the dogs to the *qamutiik* with all our packed gear and charged over to the plane. Suulut was there to see us off, he helped Danny unlash the rope bindings on the *qamutiik* so it could be dismantled and fit in the aircraft. Tom Kiguktak from Grise Fiord had come on the plane for a brief visit, but the pilots hurried the proceedings as they had a report that the weather might close in at Grise Fiord.

In no time, we were all on board, the engines roared, and the plane took off smoothly, once again packed tight with dogs and gear, along with two fifty-gallon barrels of aviation fuel in the middle of the plane. I hadn't noticed these on our flight over, and as we flew closer to Grise Fiord it became apparent why they were brought along. The co-pilot came out of the cockpit. 'Folks, bad weather in Grise, we're flying to Resolute now', he announced loudly, over the engine noise as he squeezed through our belongings and stretched over the fuel barrels to insert a hand pump. Danny and I looked at each other, dumbfounded, as he pumped more fuel into the tank. We hadn't reckoned on this contingency. I let the news sink in, preoccupied by the sight and fumes of this dangerous refuelling in mid-air manoeuvre.

How would we get back now? We didn't have the money for another flight to Grise Fiord. I had an idea and ran it past Danny sitting in front of me. 'Why don't we land on the sea ice on Jones Sound? We have everything we need for a few days to get back to Grise Fiord ourselves?'

'That's true, we have enough supplies, we could get back ourselves.'

'You have to go to Resolute to clear customs with the RCMP there', the co-pilot interjected.

'But the RCMP officer in Grise can do that.' Danny said.

'This is an international flight, folks. You must clear customs when you land. I'm sorry, but you have to go to Resolute.'

The RCMP officer in Resolute Bay gave our baggage a quick look and signed the necessary papers. Now we were stranded about 400 km away, upset that the airline had not taken us home. The agreement, we argued, was to bring us to Grise Fiord, and there had been no mention of customs clearance in Resolute, so they must fly us back now that the official business was done. They agreed to fly us back, but we had to pay. Even the regularly scheduled flight was expensive. Most of their charter business involved researchers and scientists with big budgets flying to remote areas of the Arctic through the Polar Continental Shelf Project, and when additional costs arose, there was no quibbling, but we had no extra money for unforeseen events. Reluctantly, we sold our Spilsbury Tindall radio to a local outfitter and used the money we had set aside for our return journey to Ireland to pay for the charter from Greenland as well as buy the tickets to Grise Fiord. The next day, after camping overnight on the beach, we were back home.

Chapter Fourteen

To spread out in our house in Grise Fiord again after weeks of camping on ice was a luxury, though short-lived. The community buzzed with energy following months of winter life. Skidoos and qamutiit crisscrossed the shimmering expanse of sea ice at all hours, filling the air with excitement. Everyone was on the move, embracing the season for staying out on the land when hunting and fishing took precedence over any other activity, and no one stayed at home if they could be camping at one of their favourite fishing lakes or hunting on the ice in the fiords.

The bustle was infectious – we had to join in. First, to celebrate Orla's third birthday, we loaded our camping gear onto the *qamutiik*, hitched the dogs up, and set off across the sea ice to meet Meeka and other members of the Kiguktak family, who were camped at a point opposite South Cape, fifty kilometres west of Grise Fiord. The *qamutiik*, lightly laden, sliced through the sparkling snow as the sun rose higher in the sky on a light breeze. The dogs were enthusiastic, Kaiyoo leading with the longest trace, followed by Big Brother and Rambo, with flighty Minnie Mouse constantly changing her position, while sober Jake, shoulders down, pulled hard.

We arrived early and the Kiguktak family welcomed us with a warm brew of tea. Danny set up the tent while I unpacked and spread a tarp on the ice for a picnic in the early summer sunshine. After the candles were blown out on the chocolate smartie cake and everyone got a slice, Meeka suggested a short walk to see a frozen waterfall gracefully suspended from a cliff face. Being accustomed to a silent landscape, Orla was fascinated by the squawking of herring gulls on the cliff and the occasional call of Brent geese high above, returning to their old nesting sites after their winter sojourn 6,000 kilometres away. Back in Grise Fiord again, she escaped from the house twice to join the gulls down at the tidal ice crack, which had become unstable and dangerous with melting.

Going out with our dog team.

Orla on her third birthday.

We rushed out to rescue her when we saw her climbing over mounds of ice. 'I want to see the birds', she protested at being taken away.

Another time, Meeka's sister, Teevai, brought her back before we even realised she was missing. She had spotted Orla from her living room window, trotting towards the sea ice in her rubber boots and pyjamas, undeterred by the sub-zero temperatures. From that point on, our front door had to be locked – it was the only locked house in the community.

Meeka told us about a lake full arctic char, a type of salmon, about 150 kilometres away on Devon Island, where families were camped and others would soon be setting off. A trip across Jones Sound to another island, where we could 'jig' for fish through a hole in the lake ice at our leisure, sounded enticing. Tom, Meeka's brother had retrieved our caches for us, so we had plenty of supplies, and we spent all day preparing, packing food, clothes and camping gear, enough to last us for two weeks, with the intention of leaving around midnight when the sun dropped close to the horizon, lowering the temperature and firming the soft snow on the sea ice for easier travel. Loading the *qamutiik*, getting everyone ready and harnessing excited dogs always took longer than anticipated,

Camp near South Cape Fiord.

Danny untangles the dog traces.

but now, with continuous daylight, we planned to make our day thirty-six hours long, allowing us time to travel more and stop for tea breaks along the way.

Moving out onto flat ice was challenging as usual and even more so with the advancing warmer season. Chunks of pressure ice along the shoreline had grown into a formidable maze of huge, sculpted ice forms, many taller than us. Danny went ahead of the team, flicking his whip from side to side and leading the way through these obstacles. I stayed back, steering with the handlebars while the kids bounced along in the box. Once out on a level surface, we both jumped on, and we were off, thrilled to be speeding over smooth ice. The patchy fog didn't help navigation, but the temperature was a pleasant -10°c, and the dogs were running well, spurred on by our lead dog, Kaiyoo, who was on heat. They kept up a rapid pace after her, intent on catching up, but because of her longer trace they couldn't reach her. In response, she was flirty and skittish, ignoring Danny's commands. He resorted to cracking his whip in the air, shouting, 'Duck!', warning us to put our heads down as a precaution against a stray lash on the face.

The day progressed; the sun climbed the blue sky making the snow dazzle with sparkling whiteness as far as the eye could see. The rhythm of the runners keeping time with the dog's trot had a narcotic effect on me. I had to fight off the urge to put my head down on our load and close my eyes. The girls were getting bored and irritable, so to appease them I told them stories. As soon as I finished a second rendition of 'Jack and the Beanstalk', Tempy demanded it again. Cooped up in the box with her younger siblings for so long, was a lot to ask of her. I called for a break so they could stretch their legs while Danny untangled the dog's traces, a task that needed repeating frequently.

Later, out on Jones Sound, about halfway to Devon Island, we were stopped again, this time by the 'Big Crack', an annual occurrence where a wide-open lead or fracture stretches right across the sea ice from South Cape on Ellesmere Island to Cape Sparbo on Devon Island. We got off the *qamutiik* and stood looking down at the ominous black water lapping

Danny tests an ice bridge over the 'big crack' lead.

the edge of the ice, dark because sunlight couldn't penetrate the ice on top. Under our feet, the sea depth was over 1,000 metres, although its icy cover was only one to two metres thick at this time of year – a thin shell that imperceptibly moves up and down with the tides, along with currents and other dynamic forces that crack and split the surface, causing problems for us on our journey to the lake.

'How will we get across?' Tempy asked as we surveyed the three-metrewide cleavage.

'We'll find a place where it is narrower and then we'll be able to jump,' Danny said.

'No. I don't want to' she looked at me for reassurance.

'Don't worry, we're going to find a place where it's safe for all of us to cross, I promise,' I said. Although hesitant, she had no option but to trust us.

We continued travelling along the edge of the lead in search of a crossing point. Occasionally, an area with an ice bridge looked promising; to test its strength, Danny poked the handle of the whip through

155

He jumps across when it is narrow enough to cross.

it, then used his longer harpoon, which he conveniently kept tied to the side of the *qamutiik*, but they were all too soft, the harpoon slid through the ice collapsing it. We travelled several kilometres before we reached a point where it narrowed enough to cross.

'Look Tempy, here is easy for the dogs to jump.' Danny brought her to the edge of the narrow lead aand she was satisfied that we could go across. He then jumped it ahead of the dogs, who followed, pulling the *qamutiik*, with us onboard, and we were off again, travelling out into the middle of Jones Sound over the level compact snow coating the sea ice. Surrounded by this expansive brilliance of whiteness, with an azure sky overhead, was both calming and exhilarating, as though we were above the clouds, moving through the lower levels of the stratosphere.

'What's that black thing over there?' Danny pointed towards a dot on the ice, bringing me down to earth. 'Let's go and see.'

'I think it's a sealskin,' he said on reaching it. 'It probably fell off a hunter's *qamutiik*.'

We all got off the *qamutiik* to join him.

'Or maybe it was thrown away,' I prodded it with my foot, 'because I read there's no market for seal skins now after the ban was brought in, so they're worthless once hunters have enough for their own use.'

'Maybe,' Danny said. 'We better keep going'

'It doesn't make sense.' I helped Orla into the box. 'They have to hunt seal for their own food anyway.'

'That's what happens when people thousands of miles away make decisions and don't understand the repercussions on a small group of people.'

We jumped back on board and set off again. I was aware of the anti sealing campaigns led by celebrities such as the French actress Brigitte Bardot, who, along with Greenpeace, drew public attention in the late 1970s. But what I didn't know until I read an article in a northern newspaper in Grise Fiord was that in 1983 the EEC banned the importation of sealskins, which destroyed the market and had a huge impact on the livelihood of the Inuit who use it as a by-product, much like leather and wool. Later, in 2009, the EU continued this ban but made an exception for indigenous hunters like the Inuit, recognising that they hunt only a small number in a sustainable manner. However, by then, the global demand for seal furs had declined. In 2014, Greenpeace apologised to the Inuit for its role in causing them 'decades of grief and hardship'. It is ironic that the western world tolerates the animal cruelty associated with factory farming to produce our meat, when at least the animals hunted by indigenous people are free to live their lives in the wild.

As we got closer to Devon Island, the sky clouded over, and a light snow fell. While the children slept, my head nodded down to my chest several times, to immediately jolt upright as I was about to fall off. We were groggy from lack of sleep; the dogs were slowing down too. I watched their ten upright feather duster tails, like windscreen wipers swishing the snow, it was hard to see anything else in the enveloping whiteness. Then, without warning, the runner on the left side sank down through soft snow, revealing an open lead of water beneath us and the *qamutiik* toppled on its side. I was thrown onto my back with Oisín in my

The qamutiik *falls into a lead.*

amauti, flailing like an overturned turtle trying to get upright as seawater started to trickle into the box. Danny, thinking we were about to sink to the bottom of the sea, jumped off and grabbed the girls, then pulled my arm and hauled me out. But the lead was narrow, and the handlebar had caught on ice on the far side wedging the *qamutiik*, which gave us time to get out and rapidly retrieve the sleeping bags before they got wet. Then on command the dogs dragged the qamutiik out of the water. This time the girls didn't make a fuss, they weren't hurt or wet– a potentially serious situation at subzero temperatures. Some clothes were damp, so we stopped and pitched the tent to dry them and get some sleep. We found the perfect place in the lee of an enormous, elegant iceberg with a tall steeple.

The twenty-four-hour sun circled high in the sky, dipping lower at midnight before rising again. It was disorienting, Danny and I hadn't had any sleep for at least thirty-six hours or more and I was still tethered to the twenty-four-hour clock, even though telling the time was less relevant now. We slept well, confident that a polar bear would be scented by the dogs, giving us ample warning to grab the loaded gun which Danny kept beside him in the tent, should one amble near us. After a breakfast of porridge, we were ready for the journey once more. Closer to Devon Island, Danny spotted Cape Sparbo and we turned west. Later, he saw the scramble of ice blocks at a river's mouth – a crucial landmark leading to the fishing lake. This confusion of ice where the river meets the sea slowed us, and a strong wind blew against us, making us all miserable, but once through, travelling along the frozen river, though skiddy, wasn't demanding. An hour later, the lake came into view, and the dogs surged forward, making a straight line across the ice for the tents at the far end. I grabbed the front brake, ready to stop, while Danny pressed his foot on the back brake, a piece of metal attached to the back end of the runner. He brandished the whip yelling 'Whoa,' as he snapped it in the air, while I pressed the front brake into the ice, but I couldn't get any purchase on the rock-hard surface; it merely skittered along the side of the runner.

'Push down on the brake,' he shouted.

'I'm trying.' I pushed with all my strength, and it etched the top of the ice, slowing our speed a little. The dogs made for a large canvas tent pitched right on the lake. Danny jumped off, whipping them back and forcing them to a halt. With all this commotion, Jopee Kiguktak and his partner Elisapee emerged from the tent, amused at our rowdy arrival, and invited us in for tea. They had arrived over a week before us and had caught a lot of fish.

The dogs were content to rest as we went inside to the warm, bright interior. Danny secured them with the brake firmly embedded in the ice. A kettle steamed on the Coleman stove, and Elisapee, with baby Vanessa in the *amauti* on her back, put char on the frying pan for us. I moved with the children to sit on a snow sleeping platform draped in caribou skin at the far end. With so many bodies inside a tight space, I didn't notice the large hole in the ice floor near the platform and almost stumbled into it. Jopee had ingeniously drilled a fishing hole, about thirty centimetres in diameter, right inside the tent so he could fish from the comfort of his bed. As we watched the fish swim below us, I made sure the kids stayed safely up on the platform, nervous at the possibility of a child slipping through and becoming trapped beneath the ice.

The perfect place to camp under an iceberg.

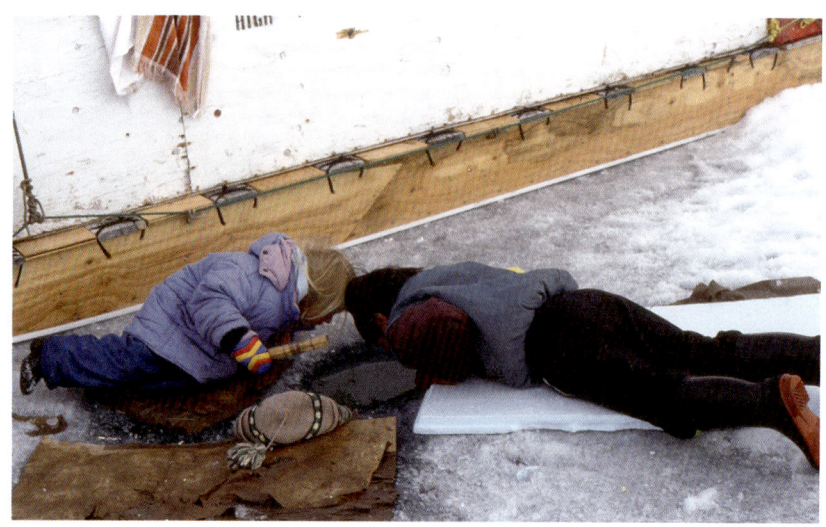

Orla fishing with Moosha.

'It's great to see the way you handle those dogs,' Elisapee said. 'No other white people came here with a dog team, and with children too.'

After a hearty feed of fish, we exited to make our own camp, unaware of the disaster awaiting us outside.

'What the hell is going on?' Danny bounded towards the dogs who had been banqueting on their own feast by stealthily pulling our *qamutiik* closer and closer to Jopee's carefully stowed stash of fish hidden beneath his upturned *qamutiik*. In embarrassment, he whipped them back, cursing them. Jopee accepted the theft with equanimity, and seeing how put out we were by the incident, offered us a snow goose he had shot that day.

We pitched our tent at the edge of the lake alongside other tents and, conveniently, several fishing holes were already bored in the ice. Teevai took Orla off to fish with her, and Danny helped Larry make more holes, a two-person task to keep the auger upright. Unlike sea ice, the ice on lakes is thicker and melts more slowly due to the absence of underlying currents, so it can take quite some time to bore through over a metre of solid ice. In true Inuit fashion, a communal spirit surrounded the fishing holes; anyone can use an unoccupied hole, regardless of who created it.

Tempy fishes in comfort.

Tempy's small fish dinner.

Larry with baby Ben.

Tempy found a hole where someone had left a chair, and we set her up with a fishing lure and line attached to a stick. She sat, dangling her line down into the water below, determined to catch a fish for her dinner. Orla preferred to lie on the ice and peer in through the hole as she fished, which was my preferred method too. Lying on a piece of cardboard to insulate myself from the cold, wet ice with my head stuck in the hole, I could see the fish swimming past the hook and jigged the line to attract a bite. Orla was quite the expert at jigging and caught three sizeable char.

Tempy caught one very small 'tiddler', but they both insisted on eating their own fish for dinner. Oisín, too young to fish, joined the other kids who had made a slide on a snow slope behind the tents. He watched as they shrieked while zooming down to the lake, sitting on a plastic garbage bag. A holiday mood spread throughout the camp; the fishing was relaxed, with plenty of sharing of country foods. Danny plucked and cleaned the goose that Jopee had given us, then I boiled it but discarded the crop (an enlarged part of the bird's oesophagus, where it stores food) on a piece of cardboard. Larry came over with his adopted son Ben and noticed it and asked, 'are you not going to eat that?'

'No'

'It's the best part. Do you mind if I have it?'

'Sure. Go ahead.' I was surprised anyone would want it.

'Look,' he prised the crop open with his knife, revealing the green willow buds inside, 'it's really good. Tastes like stuffing.'

I admired the Inuit capacity to eat all parts of an animal. Necessity had taught them not to be wasteful, every part of the animal had a use.

It struck me that the activities at this camp were like camps that the Inuit have used for millennia, travelling in small cooperative nomadic communities. Summer camps were an opportunity to gather and store fish and meat when it was abundant to alleviate the scarcity of the winter ahead. Now, with the availability of store-bought food, making caches of country foods is not so critical. Still, no commercially bought food could compare with any produce harvested from the land, and equally as important, it is what Inuit culture is all about. Living cooperatively and hunting to support the family and the community is what the people of Grise Fiord think about all the time. The archaeologist, Peter Shledermann wrote, 'we all share the heritage of these hunters no matter where or who we are today, we are all descendants from that way of life'. There is something very grounding about that fact and even better to experience it as we were doing.

With blue skies and sunshine every day, the weather warmed up and the snow retreated from the land, revealing patches of brown stony tundra. After ten days, our food supplies dwindled, and we needed to return to Grise Fiord. New arrivals at the lake told us that the 'big crack' across Jones Sound was now too wide to cross and the best route to avoid it was to turn inland fifty to sixty kilometres before Cape Sparbo, then round a big hill before turning north and going down to the sea ice again on the other side of the big crack. The suggestion of travelling overland for a change appealed to me, all our trips so far had been on frozen water.

The going was good on the ice, and we made fast progress towards land, where we camped and had a restful sleep despite the rising wind. Next day, the wind died down and when Danny poked his head out of the tent to check on the dogs who were quietly lying down, he saw all the snow had been blown off the rocky tundra.

'Damn. All those rocks are going to scratch the runners gouging their smooth surface. They'll be useless.' He dressed and went out to have a look around.

'There's still some patches of snow,' he said, coming back to the tent. 'I think we should fill in the bare patches with that snow to make ice bridges on the stony ground.'

'Are you sure? That's a lot of work.'

'We can try it. Otherwise, the runners will be ruined and the *qamutiik* will be really hard to pull.' He went over to the *qamutiik* to find the shovel and we went to work after we broke camp and packed up. We chopped and moved chunks of compacted snow to make a road down to the tide crack. The girls got into the spirit of the enterprise and contributed their handfuls of snow to our construction. It took hours to make but the wind had died down, the sun shone, and it felt good to be doing physical work together to solve our problem. And it did work. We got back on the sea ice without damaging the runners.

Travelling again on Jones Sound facing north, Danny pointed to depressions in the snow – bear footprints. 'They're not fresh. You can see they are filled with snow crystals,' he said stopping the dogs for a closer look. 'Polar bears like this part of the coastline where the seals haul out to bask in the sun.'

'I'd totally forgotten about bears being around here.' I scanned the ice for any movement. 'I'm going to keep watch now along the coast.' I kept alert, sitting on the *qamutiik* studying small icebergs that bears like to climb for a better view. Thus occupied, from the corner of my eye, I caught sight of Orla falling out of the *qamutiik* as we bounced over a lump of ice.

'Whoa, Orla overboard!' I shouted.

The dogs were almost unstoppable, racing ahead trying to catch the desirable Kaiyoo on her long lead. I kept watch behind, as Danny slowed them down, Orla growing smaller in the huge white expanse, a delicious polar bear snack. When the dogs finally halted, they reluctantly turned around and we ran to pick her up.

'Are you okay?' I asked, but I could see she was completely unfazed by the sight of her family receding into the distance.

'My feet are cold!' she said, making no fuss about the fall.

'Here, put them on my tummy and that'll warm them.' Danny opened his parka, pulled up his fleece top and the layers underneath, and put Orla's feet against his warm skin. She loved this human hot water bottle diversion, it always cheered her up, even when her feet weren't cold.

As our journey progressed out in the middle of the sound, the wind strengthened. My green gaberdine *amauti*, which had been so warm during the previous sunny days, became as flimsy as netting; the wind went right through, chilling me to the bone. Berating myself for packing away my caribou skin *amauti* too soon in the *qamutiik*, I hopped off to run beside the dogs, but I was left behind, unable to keep up. Once again, I had to ride onboard.

The gale blew harder and we made camp early. Tent pegs are useless for securing a tent on sea ice; instead, we had to make two holes in the ice, close together, forming an ice bridge between them at the points where the tent pegs would go. Then the ties and guy-lines were pushed under the bridge and secured. Danny had also sewn an apron around the bottom of the fly sheet. With some help from the girls, I shovelled snow around the tent and piled it on this apron to anchor it down, while he

Orla watches Danny cut up the seal for the dogs.

Rescuing Minnie Mouse from the sea.

stacked our supply boxes around it for extra protection. During the night, angry gusts of wind pushed and thumped against the walls of the tent, convincing me in my half-sleep that a polar bear was intruding. After a restless night, the storm continued to batter the tent, confining us for another endless day of playing games, telling stories and trying to keep the kids amused in a tight space.

The following morning, in calm stillness, we were woken by the sound of a skidoo. Etuk and Lydia were on their way to the lake. Coming into the tent, Etuk sniffed, 'I smell gas. Your stove is still on.'

I checked the knobs, 'no it's turned off.'

'Are you sure the smell of gas is strong? I think there's something wrong with your stove.'

They declined tea as they wanted to arrive early, having only a day to fish. Although I couldn't get any smell, and the stove looked fine, after they had left, as I prepared to turn it on for breakfast, I remembered a small lever hidden near the back that operates like a choke when you light it. I never used this, but the children must have turned it on while we slept, and it was now leaking white gas vapour. No wonder Etuk and Lydia didn't want to stay in the tent for tea.

Before they left, Etuk gave Danny a seal he had shot on the way here. It was a big male stinker – perfect for hungry dogs.

With well-fed dogs and hard, glassy sea ice burnished by the wind, we made good speed home, with no mishaps apart from Minnie Mouse having to be rescued from falling into a lead.

Chapter Fifteen

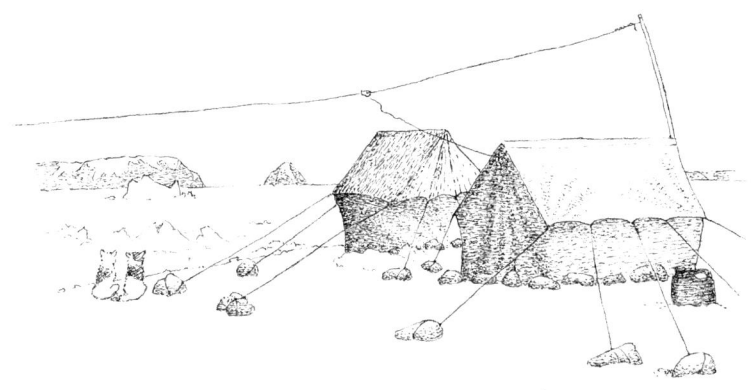

Thick fog enveloped the village as Danny and I went out to prepare to travel to Tuktu Bay, a popular hunting camp forty-five kilometres to the east of Grise Fiord. We waited until 3.00 a.m. for the low tide to drain the deep pools that formed on the ice along the shore, leaving Oisín sleeping in the house while Tempy and Orla lay awake in bed listening to story tapes. Outside, nothing stirred; it was eerie with no one about; most people were already out on the land. 21 June, midsummer, and the sun circled the sky without setting, while the strong pull of the full moon tide had shifted huge ice blocks, rearranging them and creating crevasses on our usual route through the shore ice. To get the dog team out over these obstacles was tricky.

Danny led in front, with me at the rear, steering the handlebars, but it became impossible, so we tried an alternative route near the RCMP station, where the ice appeared smoother. All went well until we reached the ice foot, a platform of sea ice locked onto the beach near the hunters' and trappers' building. A fast-flowing stream cut a deep crack in this ice foot, and it had widened enormously, forcing us to redirect the dogs to a section narrow enough to cross. Complicating matters, Minnie Mouse and Kahunga were now on heat, so all the dogs were hyped up. They leapt across the stream, yanked the handlebars from my grasp, and collided with a massive ice block, flipping the *qamutiik* over. It landed upside down in the crack.

'Shit! How did that happen?' Danny said, trying to move the sledge, but it wouldn't budge. 'Right outside town too! We'll have to carefully unload and see if we can try to drag it out.'

With the upturned *qamutiik* firmly wedged over the stream, we retrieved packs that were accessible, but the dogs still couldn't pull it out. Danny lay on his back to examine underneath.

'The harpoon's stuck in the ice, jamming it.' He tried to shift it, but it wouldn't move. I located the ice axe and he chopped furiously, dislodging the harpoon. Then we heaved the *qamutiik*, pushing it upright, and the dogs finally pulled it out. A corner of the box that carried the children looked a little damaged, but otherwise, it was fine, and all our camping gear was dry.

'I have to run and get the kids. We've been out here too long. They'll be in a state.' I rushed off, leaving Danny to repack.

To my relief, all was quiet at home. Tempy and Orla were playing outside, and Oisín was still asleep. When we got back to Danny, he was regaling Piuatuk with details of the collision.

'… I lay on the ice, peering into the crack to see if anything had been left and an almighty bang went off as a big chunk of ice, about five metres by two metres, collapsed. I loaded up and got away pretty fast,' he laughed. Tempy was not impressed. She looked disdainfully at the damaged box and refused to get in because it was 'broken'. Danny and Piuatuk mended it to her satisfaction and off we went. It was now 5.00 a.m. and the day was already getting warm.

Splashing through melted snow on the ice.

Time for refreshments.

We set the tent up on the ice.

The children fell asleep, but the dogs only wanted to fight over the females on heat and had little interest in pulling. Danny's seal skin whip softened and broke in the wet snow, and he had to resort to shouting commands. With lots of fights and tangles on the way, it was hard work, constantly jumping off the *qamutiik* to call them in the right direction. Five hours later, we arrived at Lee Point, but our destination, Tuktu Bay, lay further to the north-east. Having crossed a big lead close to the shore without difficulty, we then had to contend with lakes of surface water and the dogs would not pull. Danny and I jumped off to shove and push the *qamutiik* through huge, unavoidable melt pools. Closer to midday, the area ahead flooded with a thin snow cover on top of the water. We were getting wet, and our progress was too slow, so we turned back to Lee Point.

With the change to a homeward direction, the dogs had no problem pulling so we got back there in half the time. I put the stove on the ice beside the *qamutiik* and melted snow for hot chocolate and snacks, then woke the kids while Danny settled the dogs.

'Let's leave the dogs and *qamutiik* here and we can walk over the rough ice there towards land to find a route for them.' He pointed towards a brown patch of tundra. 'Tom showed me this site last year, his family always camp here.' We had hoped to link up with Tom's family, the Kiguktaks, who were camped somewhere in this area, but we didn't see any sign of them.

Most of the snow on the land had melted and the children played scrambling around piles of rocks, discovering ancient, petrified bones from bears, whales and seals, as well as fresh bones from more recent hunting, scattered around the empty tundra. When he put Oisín in my *amauti*, as we were leaving, Danny noticed in Oisín's fist, a bone that he was attempting to stuff down inside. He pulled it out, and on closer inspection, it turned out to be an old harpoon head. Oisín did not want to surrender it, so an exchange was made for another bone lying on the ground.

We put everything back, left them where they were found, and returned to the dogs lying on the ice.

'What's wrong with Ben?' Danny went over to the dejected dog to check him out. 'Damn, his back leg is injured.'

'Rambo!' he yelled at Rambo basking in the glory of his feuding prowess. 'He always goes for the legs. So annoying, it can put a dog out of action for some time.'

'Iglu is limping too', I pointed to his blood-stained front left foot.

Fighting over females. Big Brother's injured feet.

'They've been fighting over the females and looks like Blackie's foot is also injured. This is serious – if they can't pull the *qamutiik*'

We set the tent up on the ice, fed the dogs, then ate our freeze-dried dinners and slept in the late afternoon sunshine.

The following day, as the shadows lengthened, we reverted to our twenty-four-hour clock and slept at 'night'. In the morning, we woke to the sound of skidoos approaching and quickly dressed as the Akeeagok family pulled up beside our tent. Jaypetee, Anne, PJ, Russell, Manasie, Pauline, Ooleesie and David called in for a brief visit on their way home. They had been hunting seal over by the Jakeman Glacier, and Jaypetee gave Danny some of his catch for a small dog feed, then they needed to keep going. We waved them off, amazed to see ten-year-old Russell and Manasie driving their full-size skidoos, adept at avoiding the challenging cracks and pools of water.

As the day progressed, the sea ice became wetter than ever, forcing us to move camp onto dry land. I brought the children through the pressure ice – they were practised now at avoiding the cracks. Then, I went back to take the handlebars to steer the *qamutiik* over the ice hurdles. This time, we did it easily. I set up camp while Danny took the dogs out again in search of a seal, and the children climbed rocks looking for treasure; a broken snow bunting's egg was Tempy's prize find.

Danny hadn't been out long when I saw him returning. I grabbed the camera to catch him weaving around the ice jumble at the tide crack, which was now filling up fast with sea water. As soon as they reached the ice foot, the dogs charged towards me, throwing the *qamutiik* up on a rock. Danny shouted at them, lashing his repaired whip over their heads, subduing their enthusiasm, and they came in quietly.

'We went about eight kilometres, it was wet, and the only seal I saw was hauled out towards Tuktu Bay, over there, near deep melt pools,' he said, securing the *qamutiik* before untying the dogs.

'How did you manage the big lead?'

'I jumped it first and called the dogs. Iglu fell in and went for a swim, but on the way back they all got over it.'

Scrambling among rocks.

Danny takes the dogs out in search of a seal.

In the afternoon, we walked along the tundra searching for ducks through pools and mud from melting snow. Orla wanted to eat duck and Danny brought his rifle. In the distance, we saw two groups on a pond, but I was glad they flew off before he could get within range. We turned back with Orla complaining, 'I don't want to go home. I want to eat ducks.' Then Tempy fell into a shallow stream, getting wet legs and joined Orla crying.

Back at our camp, they immediately forgot their woes and had fun climbing rocks again and making houses with them. In the tent, as I prepared a meal of freeze-dried bean stew, much easier than having to clean out a duck or two, I heard Orla screeching, 'my eyes, my eyes'. I hurried out to find her rubbing her eyes and crying loudly. I knew immediately she had snow blindness. After all my efforts to ensure we wore sunglasses while being outside to prevent this from happening, I had been careless and let my guard down. She had hardly worn her sunglasses all day on the brown tundra where the snow had melted, but the reflection of UV light off the nearby snow on the sea was enough to cause sunburn to the sensitive surface of her eyes.

Now, she was in a lot of pain, and I was annoyed with myself. I brought her into the tent to protect her from further UV light exposure and checked our first aid kit for a suitable painkiller. She hated being imprisoned and made several attempts to escape despite my attempts to distract her with games and stories. We stayed in the tent for hours while she sobbed inconsolably. Eventually, exhaustion took over, and she slept. When she woke much later, she was back to her cheerful self and was allowed out again – wearing sunglasses.

The next morning brought more bad luck for Orla. Upon waking, we found three dogs were loose, and bundles of caribou hair were strewn around the *qamutiik*.

'What the hell! Orla's caribou pants are gone, only the cloth waistband and braces are left.' I gathered up the remains of the pants, along with clumps of caribou hair.

Orla slept in the tent.

Orla's chewed up pants.

'I bet it was Kaiyoo, she's an escape artist. I wonder what else she chewed.' Danny said opening the food box and rummaging through it. 'At least she didn't go for the food, it's all good in there. Let's check the rest of the fur clothes'

'Your mitts look a bit chewed, but not too bad.' I searched through all our caribou clothes stored in the *qamutiik*. 'Nothing else amiss here. Oh well, at least Orla won't be needing those pants again now that summer is here.'

'That dog is smart, she cleverly avoided the food in the boxes next to the tent because the noise would wake us and instead went to the *qamutiik* to eat our fur clothes,' Danny laughed.

minnNonchalant, Kaiyoo or the 'Greenland Houdini' as Danny called her, was back in her position on the dog line, but her rope tether was chewed through, and final proof of the theft came hours later when she produced a twisted rope of furry shit.

After five days away, I needed to get back to 'Grise' to mail some photos to the *Sunday Tribune* newspaper, but we stayed another day so Danny could paint. He had scant opportunity during our travels and on a warm, sunny day, I needed little persuasion. The kids were content with their game of making snow sculptures on the ice beside him.

By the time he finished his painting and we had eaten and packed up, it was 2.00 a.m., a good time to travel with the sun low in the sky, but the shore pressure ice had grown higher and tilted to a steeper angle, so it took nearly an hour to get through it all. When we came to the widened lead stretching from Lee Point far out to the south-east, the dogs crossed with only Iglu, Ben and Minnie Mouse swimming again. We pulled them out, they gave their thick coats a thorough shake, and off we went as they steamed the moisture off their coats in the subzero temperature. Melt pools and wet snow slowed our progress and it was around 9.00 a.m. by the time we arrived back. Annie Audlaluk saw us and took the kids to the shore, while Danny and I guided the dogs and *qamutiik* to dry land. Larry gave Danny half a seal for the dogs, and Jimmy Kapik added some offal so they were well-fed; he also gave us some seal meat for our dinner.

Tempy and Oisín make a snow rocking horse sculpture.

Minnie Mouse falls in again.

We were only home a few days when Danny suggested we go out 'egg-hunting'. At this time of year, gulls nested on the steep cliffs to the west of the village and their eggs were highly rated by the Inuit. The weather was calm, clear and warm and soon the ice would be gone – a good excuse for a trip along the coastline. Tempy had enough of travelling on the qamutiik and stayed playing with her friend Adeline. In this tight-knit community, we didn't have to worry about leaving her behind as everyone looked out for each other's children. While walking with Orla and Oisín down to the jumbled sea ice where the dogs were staked out, Danny noticed Jaypetee and Raymond arriving, towing a small boat laden with meat on their qamutiik. They were returning from hunting at the floe edge. He waited to help them push the qamutiik over the ice floes, and soon lots of people came to assist. The first landing of 'maktaaq', the black and white mottled skin of the narwhal, a highly prized treat, was exciting and everyone wanted a share.

Jaypetee fed our dogs big chunks of whale meat, not knowing they had been well-fed the previous night, and they still devoured all the fresh meat he threw to them. Then Danny harnessed eight dogs, leaving Big Brother and Blackie behind with injured feet, and we headed out on this warm sunny day. But, after their big feed, the dogs had no energy to pull, and Danny had to crack the whip all the time or run ahead calling them. They didn't want to work. At one stage, they almost turned the *qamutiik* over while running alongside a small lead, tipping me off onto the ice. Kaiyoo, was totally distracted and refused to pay attention. Danny attempted to nip her with the whip, but she hid among the other dogs. When he pulled her out, she escaped and ran up in front to the full length of her rope, her usual position, howling all the time even though he had not used the whip on her. The effort of trying to reprimand her eventually paid off as she became more attentive to obeying commands.

By the time we got to the point, a few kilometres away, they were running better. We stayed close to the coast, going around and through deep pools of water, my kamiks got soaked and everything on the *qamutiik* was getting splashed. I was busy checking that none of the pools were dark and bottomless, when David Akeeagok came behind us on his skidoo. He said his mother, Ooleesie, wanted to make cheese, so he was going out to get a seal.

'How do you make cheese from a seal?' I asked.

'Chop it up and sew it into the seal skin, then bury it under stones and leave it for about six months. It's called *igunaq*".'

'Oh, it ferments.' I wasn't disappointed that I wouldn't be around to taste it. At least Ooleesie used the traditional method of making it and didn't enclose it in modern materials such as plastic bags to ferment it, which is a botulism risk.

We came to a recently arrived herring gull colony on the red granite cliffs. Over many generations, the birds had abandoned the lower ledges and kept out of reach of egg thieves by nesting higher up. Danny tried climbing, but the rock was too steep and flaky, so we went on a bit further. David came back and we invited him to have tea. I melted snow from the top of the sea ice which made horrible salty tea. Danny and I spat it out, but David politely finished his. Then Danny and David tried to climb to another nest, reaching up to thirty metres before retreating because of loose holds.

'It's very freaky when you are high up to find your holds rattling around,' Danny said.

'You shouldn't be taking those risks.'

'Let's try the next colony down the fiord, it's about ten kilometres away.'

'But you don't have ropes or climbing gear, it's too risky.' In truth, I was also worried about the condition of the melting sea ice. David told us it was rotting in places further on with holes going right through it. Orla made the final decision for us. She woke and started crying, complaining she was cold, even though it was a warm day. We failed to pacify her, so we packed up the stove and headed homeward. Closer to the community, we met a group of giggling women fishing in an ice crack.

'Orla, come fish with us' Annie Audlaluk called, and Orla immediately perked up at this invitation.

'What are you catching?' Danny asked.

'Kanajuq, ugly fish,' Mary Flaherty said, showing him her catch of sculpin, small fish with large heads and not much meat. 'We're just having fun. It's Canada Day. You should go to the airstrip, there's games and food for everyone.'

Celebrations were in full swing when we arrived at the emergency airstrip; fires had been lit using old packing crates, with pots of seal stew and hot dogs sizzling over the flames, and a huge cake, iced with 'Happy Birthday Canada' in red and white as the centrepiece on a small table. There were bike races for kids, three-legged and six-legged races, and a spider-collecting contest, which required the utmost bravery since many Grise Fiord people have a deep fear of insects, including those intrepid hunters who have no difficulty facing polar bears. Danny gathered twelve

Danny scales the cliffs looking for gulls' eggs.

hiding under stones but he was outdone by the intrepid Rynee Flaherty, who won the prize with thirteen spiders. I was amazed that spiders could survive in this environment. Apparently, they have evolved not to freeze to death in the winter by lowering their metabolism and producing glycol, a type of antifreeze that prevents ice forming around their bodies or allows ice to form only outside their cell walls. Now, with climate change causing longer, warmer summers in the Arctic, spiders are enjoying an extended reproduction time, leading to a spider baby boom, which could have other effects on this ecosystem over time.

Chapter Sixteen

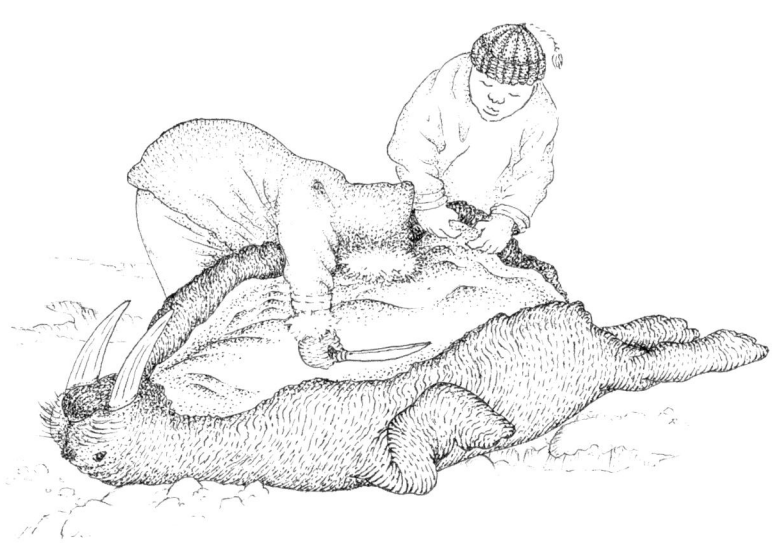

The melting of the sea ice accelerated in July and Danny fretted about his diminishing chances of taking the dogs out on painting trips, he was determined to keep going out for as long as he could, despite the formidable obstacles of open water and fragile ice. I thought he was crazy to attempt to bring the dog team through a puzzle of disintegrating ice fragments, but I helped him with the preparations for his solo trip. While he made a box with scrap wood to secure a large canvas for painting onto the qamutiik, I got his food, utensils, and spare clothes together and wrapped everything in plastic bags to protect them from the inevitable saltwater splashing they would get. By 6.30 a.m. at low tide, he was ready to go. With Oisín in my amauti, I went down to the beach to help him get the dogs over the water-filled ice foot.

'I'm going to leave Big Brother, Blackie, Ben and Kahunga, because they still have sore feet with cuts from the sharp ice,' he said.

'Will six dogs be enough?'

'Yeah, the *qamutiik* is light. I've very little on it.'

I held the excited bunch of dogs while he pushed the *qamutiik* over the tide cracks to form a bridge. Crossing over he called them to follow, but they refused to use the bridge or swim. Then he tried to drag Rambo over by tying the end of the whip to his harness and pulling, but he would not budge. With Oisín on my back and a melee of dogs on traces around me, I was nervous I would be pulled into the water. Eventually, reliable Jake, Danny's favourite dog swam over, and the others followed or got pulled in. He hitched them to the *qamutiik*, and led them meandering through narrow sloping ice mounds and ponds with deep holes at the bottom, keeping up some speed to stop the *qamutiik* from sliding in. Even so it took two hours to get through a kilometre of this pressure ice. Having watched two hunters, Charlie and Levi, in difficulty setting out the day before, with Levi turning his skidoo over in a crack, he was relieved that it was not as bad as he had anticipated.

Out on Jones Sound, the surface was better; the meltwater had drained, but in its place, razor-sharp ice crystals had formed during the night, lacerating the dogs' feet. Iglu developed a limp, and Rambo left a trail of bloody paw prints on the snow. He put boots on their injured feet, and they started pulling again. On approaching a group of small islands, broad leads full of black water appeared; one, ten metres wide, required a long detour. 'It was worth it,' he said, recounting the whole journey later, 'because otherwise, I wouldn't have spotted a seal basking on the ice in the distance. I stalked it from behind my white hunting screen and shot it.' He now had fifty kilos of fresh meat for the dogs.

When he reached the first little island, the Skerries, he set up camp and began to paint a large canvas in acrylics, thinly, like a watercolour. 'After the first few hours painting, I was ecstatic,' he said, 'it was simple, almost Zen-like. But I chickened out of leaving it like that and worked it up a bit.' While he painted, the sea ice rose with the tide, elevating

Iglu wearing booties.

Danny's camp next to the skerries.

Danny stalking a seal.

Coming home, Danny's last trip with the dogs.

his camp to the level of the island's peak, then down again, by five to six metres every six hours – all the while, the enormous blocks of ice surrounding the island creaked and cracked. He preferred to paint at 'night-time' when the sun was lower. 'But I had to keep stuffing the canvas into the tent with the stove going to dry each wash and unfreeze it,' he said, 'even the water in the ice cracks froze each night.'

The place was alive with birds. 'Up to 200 Arctic Terns in the sky, all squawking and occasionally threatening to dive bomb me. Pintail and Eider ducks swam in the cracks around the Island – they would suddenly shoot over my head quacking excitedly,' he reminisced. 'Ivory gulls and Herring gulls came to share some of the seal meat. And a few times a long-tailed Arctic Skua would chase a tern, screeching violently until the tern vomited up its food, which was caught in the air and devoured by the skua.'

After three days of painting, he noticed threatening lenticular clouds forming to the south over Devon Island and although he hadn't much sleep, he packed up in case a big storm was coming and set off towards

Grise Fiord. As he glided over smooth ice thinking how strange and lovely it was to be travelling on a frozen sea in the middle of July, his daydreams were interrupted when suddenly he saw the dogs swimming in a big lead. They had run into the crack at an angle, and he barely had time to jump off, shove the *qamutiik* straight and leap on again. The front of the runners caught on the far side, so he scrambled on with his weight balancing the back end. The dogs managed to climb out of the water and pull the *qamutiik* out and they were off again at a gallop. He didn't want to miss low tide to get off the ice – but it was already coming in by the time they arrived near town and the pools were deep. For one stretch, he had to unhitch the dogs and steer the *qamutiik* over small ice floes . At another crack, he bridged it with the *qamutiik* and crossed, dragging the dogs after him. Some preferred to swim and had to be pulled out, unable to scale the height of the ice on the other side, and this whole escapade excited them so much that they took off at top speed without Danny, ignoring his shouts to stop. Miraculously, they only got about eighty metres before half-sinking the *qamutiik* which brought them to an abrupt halt.

Sensing his anger, when Danny reached them, they focused on pulling with huge effort and the *qamutiik* slid out of the hole. He caught the handlebars and turned the *qamutiik* over on its side so they couldn't run off again, the brake having been torn off. Still giddy with excitement they refused to turn back onto the only route in. The ice was now broken into small floating rafts a metre or two across and the old route was totally open water. From the house, I saw him having difficulty and went out with the kids to try to direct him in, but eventually, he decided the only way to do it was to free each dog and let them find their own way in. They bounded from floe to floe to dry land, where I captured them and clipped them on the stake out chain.

As I caught the dogs, two managed to escape. Tempy's friend, Pauline, backed off in fright, calling the children after her. Meanwhile, Danny pushed the *qamutiik* over the floating ice, and we dragged it up to the ice foot on the beach. The escapees were caught and secured onto their chain – a fitting end to their final adventure with us. Danny was the last to get in without using a small boat or kayak. Over the next week, we watched the hunters with fascination as they came and went back and forth across the widening channel between the sea ice and the land, using small boats to reach their skidoos parked on the ice, from where they could still access their hunting grounds.

Jaypetee returned from the floe edge, having been out hunting for a week. The tide was well in with about 100 metres of water separating land from sea ice. A few skidoos were still parked on the ice on the far side of this stretch of water. As soon as he parked his skidoo next to a line of other snowmobiles, the ice edge gave way, and it disappeared into the depths. He tried fishing it out with poles, but it was never seen again. He didn't seem upset by the loss, even though he had only just bought it from a teacher, and no one had insurance here. These things happen, Inuit say, and being angry doesn't make it easier, it would be worse if a person had gone under.

In the short grey midnight dusk, Luti and Jimmy Qappik hunted walrus right in front of our house. One huge walrus raised its head in the water, clearly visible without binoculars. We didn't see them catch it, but we got a share of the meat. I insisted we boil it because of the risk of trichinosis which the older male walruses sometimes carry, but it was tough, so the dogs enjoyed it instead.

Rising about 10.00 a.m. the next morning to have the quiet house to myself while everyone slept, I put the kettle on for tea, then the front door opened and Tempy sauntered in.

'Tempy!' I almost dropped the kettle. 'Where were you, I thought you were asleep in bed?'

'I was playing with my friends.' She staggered with tiredness.

'You were out all night! I can't believe it. You're only six, you can't stay out all night!' I helped her take her jacket off. 'Go to bed now, you're tired.'

'I'm not tired, I'm bored, I'm not tired.' She cried hysterically. I coaxed her to her bed, helped her undress, tucked her in and she quickly fell asleep. Berating myself for my carelessness in not checking she was in bed, I realised the lack of routine, waking, sleeping, and eating at any hour of the day or night was making life complicated. Her friends seemed to prefer to sleep by day and play in the midnight shade, and for hunters, it makes sense to sleep by day when hunting is easier in the cooler twilight night, but now that we were back home again, I wanted my old routine.

During this time of being confined to land, there was a lot more activity around the settlement, with people coming and going to visit each other. Tookillkee's sister, Parnee, had just arrived in Grise Fiord, and Danny invited her in for a cup of tea. She told me she was returning to live in the community. 'I just came up here to see my brother,' she said as we chatted around the kitchen table. 'I hadn't seen him for twenty years and I decided to stay.'

'You must like Grise Fiord then?'

'Yeah, it's quiet, and I get a chance to go out hunting. I don't get to do when I'm in different settlements.'

She told me that for many years, she had spent every summer working as an interpreter on the *CD Howe*, a Canadian government ship that visited eastern Arctic communities in the 1950s and 1960s to provide medical and dental services, deliver supplies and increase the government's presence in the region.

'I loved that job, I got to visit every community in the eastern Arctic from Labrador to Baffin Island and sometimes right up here in Grise Fiord. We had doctors and dentists on board as well as nurses and interpreters. And X-ray equipment, mostly screening for TB. It was really well equipped, like a mobile hospital'.

Parnee was enthusiastic about her experience of the *CD Howe*, which was quite a contrast to other stories I had heard about this ship. Anne's mother, Margaret, who lived in many different communities on Baffin Island, told me people would run away and hide when the ship appeared on the horizon, suspecting they would be forced against their will to go down south to hospital, sometimes never to be seen again by family and friends if they died there.

'People who tested positive for TB were kept on board, for fear they would run away and hide if they were allowed back to their homes,' Margaret told me. 'They had to go down to the TB sanatorium in Montreal for treatment. And they were away for a very long time, often many years. Families didn't understand what happened when people disappeared, there was no communication. One mother thought her young son had died, he was away for so many years. While he was gone, she had another baby boy whom she gave the same name as her presumed "dead" son. When the older boy had recovered and returned on the ship to his family, she rejected him. She couldn't accept he was her son.'

'That's heart-breaking – for both. What happened to him?'

'He was adopted by a family in another community.'

Every community has similar poignant stories of loss. In Grise Fiord, Mary Flaherty, aged only two years, was taken from her family and sent to a sanatorium in Manitoba, where she stayed for months. She responded well to treatment and was discharged, but because the ship only visited once in the summer, she was sent to Montreal to wait there for her return journey. Then, in the summer, the ship put her ashore in Inukjuaq, where the Flaherty family originally lived before being relocated, which is over 2,000 kilometres further south from Grise Fiord. She stayed there with relatives to wait another year for the ship to take her home, all this time her parents knew nothing of her whereabouts or when she would return. The following summer, now aged four years, she went onboard only to be taken off at Resolute Bay, again the wrong community, where she spent a further year with another family. Finally, after three years, she was reunited with her own family in Grise Fiord, but having lost the bond with them, this transition was painful, and initially she had great difficulty settling into the strange Arctic environment that was now called home.

It was estimated that by 1956, one in every seven Inuit were in sanatoria down south. Some died and were buried there but most recovered and eventually returned to their communities.

Piuatuq watches Danny paint.

The medical authorities were so focused on eliminating this dreaded disease from communities where at least one-third of the population were infected, that they didn't recognise or consider the personal and community trauma the treatment caused. Paternalistic attitudes were common in those days. Inuit were often treated as errant children who had to be instructed. In the 1930s, when the Canadian government began to establish RCMP stations and other agencies in the Arctic, they needed to register people but found the Inuit naming system complex and difficult to pronounce, so they developed another system for identification. An identification tag or disc was introduced, stamped with numbers and letters to indicate the district the person was from and their own ID. The disc had to be worn at all times. After a faltering start, this system became widespread in the late 1940s when it was required for receipt of welfare payments and health services. It continued until 1972 and was then replaced by 'Project Surname' when Inuit were assigned surnames. Before this, their naming system did not include surnames but was exceptionally meaningful, conferring the 'atig' or 'soul name' of the person they are called after, where the child takes on that person's identity, usually a beloved dead relative. I sometimes heard an adult call their son 'Ataata' or 'Father' if the boy was given the *atig* of his grandfather. Conversely, the child might call his father 'Irniq' or 'Son'. This naming system could also explain why the mother would not accept her returned son.

Towards the end of July, the weather became more variable, sometimes clear and sunny, other times rain and fog, like an Irish winter. On one misty day with low cloud, Danny went out to paint the small icebergs marooned on the beach about four houses further along from ours, and he asked Orla to bring him some tea. Taking his request seriously, she ordered the tea as soon as he left. I packed a small backpack for her with a thermos flask, and having reassured her that there weren't any polar bears lurking about the ice, off she went, adamant that I was not to come with her. I had to resort to following discreetly, hiding between the houses. She dawdled, stopping every time she heard a dog yelp or growl to check it wasn't after her. Then she saw Piuatuk coming towards her to say hello. Ignoring him, she quickened her pace – a three-year-old on a mission.

Once she safely arrived at her destination, I turned for home. How quickly and easily the children have adapted to life here, better than me, I thought. Now that we were landbound, I craved green vegetation to rest my eyes on. The melted snow exposed a dreary brown-grey landscape of cliff, rock, and scree. Pauline told me about a grassy area nearby, and we decided to go there the next day to have a family picnic with Pauline, Susie, Adeline, Manasie, PJ and any other child who wanted to come along. It was a sunny day as we picked our way along the coastline. We brought Jake along to carry our food and Orla insisted on holding his lead. Soon, an astounding lush oasis of green appeared, nestled in among the rocks of the shore, with abundant yellow arctic poppies and purple saxifrage. A magnificent Arctic secret garden glowing with colour against a backdrop of dazzling stranded ice floes. I lay down on the greenery, luxuriating in this most unexpected exuberant vegetation while the children played sardines, hiding behind the rocks.

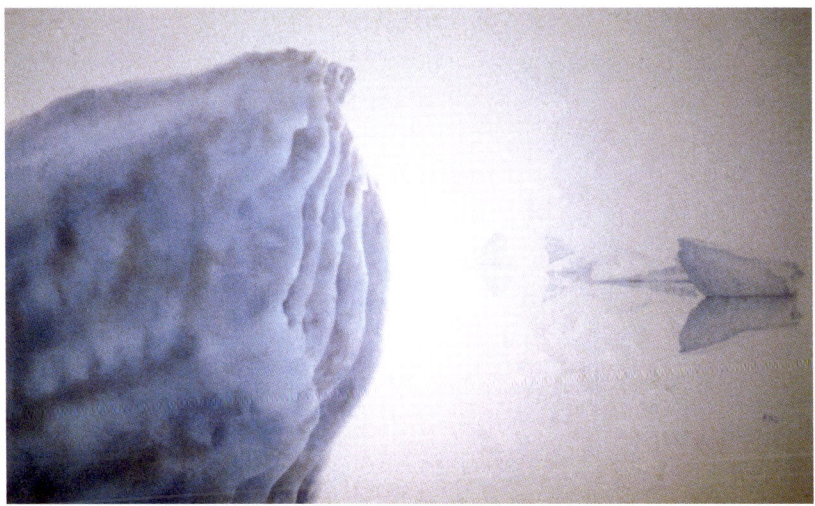

Watercolour painting of small floating icebergs.

Orla takes Jake to the picnic.

Closing my eyes, I pictured the low green hills around our home in Beara, covered with abundant purple heather and the vivid yellow of gorse in bloom at this time of year. Danny interrupted my sudden pang of homesickness by bringing up the subject of dogs, specifically our need to sell the team, as they could not be used again for another three to four months. We had vaguely discussed this previously.

'Oh yes, I almost forgot, Iga asked me about buying the dogs yesterday,' I said, opening the thermos and pouring tea into a plastic cup. 'Kiguktak wants a dog team, so I agreed, but I wasn't sure how much we should ask for?'

'What! I've already told Jaypetee he can have them'. He almost spilt the tea I handed him. 'This was arranged a couple of days ago. I told you that'

'No, you didn't. I don't remember you telling me that.'

Danny wanted to keep the team together, after all the work he had put into their training, they were now driving like a Rolls Royce, each one knowing their place in the group. We finally agreed that the only way to settle this predicament was to divide them. At least their new owners were both good hunters and would look after them well, although he was embarrassed to have only five dogs to hand over to Jaypetee.

The following day, he called to him to complete the transaction, and when the deed was done, he returned in a much better mood.

'Jaypetee and Anne are fine with the five dogs; in fact, they've invited us to come along with them to Devon Island in August. They're going to charter a plane. Apparently, Anne's job pays for one plane journey a year for the whole family, so instead of going south, they use it to go caribou hunting, and they want to know if we would like to come along, all of us. They're all going: Akeeagok, Ooleesie, Pauline … It will be a great trip. I said I would speak to you first … we ought to go.'

'Oh yes, that sounds fantastic!'

Chapter Seventeen

O ur destination on the north-western shores of Devon Island was marked on our map as an area of raised beaches dotted with lakes. We climbed aboard the Twin Otter with Anne and her kids to join the rest of the Akeeagok family, who were already there. Tents, food, and fuel were stacked at the back, and this time we had no dogs, they were being looked after by Seeglok in Grise Fiord. The small plane flew low over the dark open waters of Jones Sound, dappled with ice floes and bergs, where only weeks ago we crossed with the dog team, and then on to the boundless empty flatness of the tundra. Searching for a place to land, it circled an area of stony grey terrain before the large balloon tyres bounced over the shaley ground. Pauline ran to greet us as we disembarked; she was excited to show us where to camp. We trudged over the tundra, following her, laden with bags of supplies.

'You want some?' she asked, offering me a small white square of candy.

'Thanks', I popped the creamy white cube in my mouth and chewed it. It didn't taste sweet. 'What is it?'

'Tuktu.'

'Oh ... of course, caribou.' I should have known; we are here to hunt caribou after all. It must be the raw fat, I guessed, much better for children than the sugary confections they buy in the shop.

'Want more?' She had handfuls in her pocket.

'No thanks, I'm not hungry now. But it's very good.' Although I didn't like to admit it, knowing what it was changed my taste perception.

We pitched our tent on a raised beach close to the sea beside tthree other tents: Jaypetee, Anne, and the children in one, Ooleesie, David, Manasie, Amon, Pauline and Rhoda in the other two.

'Apparently, a polar bear was spotted around the camp last night,' Danny casually informed me, taking his boots off at the tent entrance.

Camp on Devon Island. David changes the tyre on the ATV.

'I was just over in David's tent, and he told me he chased it off on the ATV for some distance.'

'I hope it doesn't come back. There's meat all over the place, it must be very enticing.'

'There are enough people here to scare it off if it does. I wouldn't worry. Let's see what's in here to eat.' He rummaged in the food box. 'Oh … and Ooleesie says to help ourselves to the caribou meat outside. Just take whatever you want.'

'That's nice of her. I'll get some now.'

Four skinned caribou carcasses lay on cardboard and black plastic rubbish bags between our tent and Ooleesie's. The extremely dry, cold air allowed the meat to be left outside for weeks, even in the summer, without going off. With my small, blunt carving knife, I cautiously approached the nearest one, wondering if there was an etiquette regarding where to cut or which anatomical areas were valued more than others. Some slices had already been taken from a haunch, so I cut a few more slices off and brought them back to the tent. Fried lightly in butter, it was delicious. Danny insisted on having a couple of thin slices raw. 'This is the best way to eat it,' he said, trying to convince me. Outside, the girls ran around with the other children, while Oisín sat on the ATV imagining he was going places.

The next morning, I strolled up a slope at the back of the tents to check on the kids. Near the top of the rise, they rushed towards me, screaming, 'Ummingmaq, muskox, it's coming!' In the distance, I could make out a lone bull muskox, one of those shaggy prehistoric bovines (although, apparently, they are more closely related to sheep and goats, but considerably larger), his long hair streaming in the wind as he moved lazily in the opposite direction. The kids had panicked when the animal turned towards them.

'It's all right he's not coming now, he's going away.' I calmed them. PJ had fallen and cut his tummy on a sharp stone, though the thought of being left behind with a charging muskox hurt more than a small laceration. From the top, I surveyed the land spread out in a vast rolling

Anne and kids watch retreating muskox.

plain, occasionally cut by a ravine, with no visible grass, bushes, or trees and no landmarks. How do hunters find their way? I would be lost within minutes, yet they travelled across this featureless terrain for many kilometres in search of caribou herds that mainly feed on mosses and lichens.

Back at camp, Danny got ready to go caribou hunting with Jaypetee and David. They planned to be gone for several hours, needing to cover a large area on foot in search of a herd. While they were gone, I visited Anne in her tent. The wind rose, violently striking the heavy canvas sides of the tent, but inside it was cosy with the Colman stove on a low heat. Chatting with Anne, I asked her about how Inuit traditional adoptions are arranged.

'If you want to adopt a baby and you know a relative or friend who is having a baby, then you can ask, "can I adopt the baby?",' she explained.

'So, there's no legal process involved. And do the birth parents keep in touch with the child?'

'All of the children are told who their birth mother is, and they keep in contact. They always send pictures to show how the child is doing if they are living in another community.'

Eight years earlier, Ooleesie tragically lost two sons in a house fire. She was so traumatised by this horrific loss, Anne told me, that her neighbours, a young couple, decided to have a baby for her as she was then in her late forties. It took four years for a baby to arrive, and in the meantime Ooleesie had adopted other children, Pauline and Rhoda, now much-loved family members. Adoption has always been part of Inuit life; it was essential for survival – for orphans and for older parents who needed a hunter in the family.

Our hunters returned to camp later in the day carrying three caribou, skinned, cut up and tied on their backs. David took the ATV to retrieve the remaining meat they could not carry.

'Why didn't you leave all the meat in one place and then retrieve it with the ATV?' I asked Danny, who looked exhausted after his long day.

'If all the cache was left there, it could be raided by bears or wolves.'

'How far did you have to carry it?'

'Pretty far. We carried it for about four hours. Sometimes we used head straps for the heavy meat, but it hurt my forehead too much, so I preferred to tie it on my back.'

Again, I lost track of time, barely noticing each day merging into the next. Once, we set off on an exploratory walk along the coast, Danny, myself with Oisín in my amauti, and the girls, with Pauline, and PJ. Orla walked slowly so Danny put her in his rucksack, from where she could look over his shoulder. As we ambled along this raised beach area, Danny encouraged us to keep our eyes on the ground, looking for fossils. Almost every stone we picked up had either an ammonite or a small scallop-type shell imprinted on it, reminding us that this area was once under the sea between 9,500 and 5,500 years ago.

After an hour of walking, Tempy and Pauline refused to go any further; they wanted to return to the camp, but Danny was determined to press on, so we split up. He continued walking with Orla while I led the children back. We wandered along the sandy shoreline, heads down, engrossed in searching for any interesting finds from the sea. Suddenly, Pauline ran towards me shrieking, '*Aiviq. Aiviq.* Over there.' She pointed to some large boulders on the beach.

My heart leapt, a polar bear! And Danny has the gun, I forgot to get it from him. But wait, she didn't say *nanuk*?

'What is it?' I asked squinting at the rocks. 'I can't see anything.'

'Look, *aiviq*, there, he's coming. I'm scared.' She clung to my side.

Then I saw the walrus emerge from between the boulders about sixty metres away, slowly lumbering toward us.

'Oh, it's only a walrus,' I said, relieved it hadn't a white furry shape, and lingered a while to observe the bulky creature. Pauline hopped in agitation beside me, reminding me that there could be bears here too.

'Let's see how fast we can get back to the tents,' I said, gathering the kids to retreat from the beach. We were back in thirty minutes. Ooleesie was sitting outside her tent, scraping a sealskin in the sunshine. Using her *ulu,* or knife, at a low angle to the surface, I watched her separate the gooey, pink layers of oily blubber from the thin, delicate skin. It looked

Ooleesie scrapes blubber from seal skin.

easy, but I knew it wasn't, and I should have offered to help; however, I was afraid I would destroy the work she was doing.

Danny returned hours later. 'You should have come; it was amazing,' he said, releasing Orla from his backpack. 'I came across a pile of old, rusty food cans scattered about in this small depression in the ground. They all had thick, dripping lead solder. They could be from the Franklin expedition, you know, from the 1840s, because Beechy Island, where he first camped, is just to the south of us here.'

'Were they intact?'

'Yes, they were, and in fairly good condition considering how old they are. In those days, canned food had just been invented, and they didn't know about the risk of lead poisoning. Of course, they could be from a cache from some of the search parties who travelled here looking for the lost Franklin ships too.' He paused, lost in thought, and then grabbed the food box to get some cookies for Orla. 'They had plenty of food on board at that point in their expedition,' he added.

The ill-fated Franklin expedition continues to attract public interest in 2024. Scientists in Canada analysed the DNA of human remains on King William Island, identifying the bones of James Fitzjames, the Irish commander of the ship Erebus. They also discovered marks of cannibalism on his jawbone, indicating how desperate the starving crew members were. King William Island was where another Irishman, Captain McClintok (who met Qitdlarssuaq), discovered evidence of what had happened to the ships when he found the remains of some crew members in May 1859, along with a note in a cairn reporting Franklin's death, the abandonment of the iced-in ships, and the plan to travel south overland to seek help. It was also probable that many of the crew suffered from lead poisoning caused by the tinned meat.

For Inuit boys, learning to hunt starts at an early age – as soon as they can handle a rifle. By the time they reach ten, they are able to shoot rabbits (as Arctic hares are called), foxes and seals – even caribou. Anne's son Russell had already shot three caribou.

'He goes hunting whenever he can, even sometimes when he has school; hunting comes first,' she told me. 'And at school, they have this programme called "Cultural Inclusion", where the boys go out hunting.'

It was reassuring to hear that the skills of the Inuit hunters are still being passed on to the next generation, just as they always had in the past, but my approval was tested when Russell decided to do some target practice with his rifle a short distance from our camp. He set up a cardboard box as a target, and as soon as he fired, his audience of younger children, including Tempy and Orla, raced towards the target to be the first to find the bullet shell case. It was a game for them, but the risk of a mistimed shot alarmed me. I wanted to stop this activity, yet none of the adults back at the tents seemed to notice. I could take my children away, but that would not solve the risk to the other kids.

'Why don't you play a different game and leave Russell to practise his shots? It's too dangerous. I don't want you to be playing this,' I said.

Oisín plays with caribou ribs.

'It's fun.'

'We want to play this game'

I decided to lay down some rules and supervise it.

'Russell, you have to be sure to wait and check that all the children are behind you before you shoot,' I said to him.

He agreed, and I knew he was a responsible, mature ten-year-old.

'And children, listen, you must wait behind Russell until I say 'GO' before you run for the bullet case, or else you can't play.'

They followed my rules, and after a few more shots, Russell became bored and abandoned his target practice. He showed me a small wooden model *qamutiik* with a lemming skin stretched over it instead of seal skin. He made it himself, he told me, even killing the lemming and skinning it. So accomplished at only ten years old, but a few nights later, Orla was very unimpressed with his hunting skills. As twilight was setting in, she returned to the tent in a distressed state while Danny and I were dozing.

'Why did Russell kill the fox?' she demanded loudly.

'Oh, I don't know, did Russell kill a fox?' I mumbled, trying to wake up.

'Was it a bad fox?' Tears started to flow.

'Maybe, I don't know. It's time to go to bed now, you're tired.'

'It was a bad fox,' she screeched.

'Yes, it was a bad fox.' Both Danny and I agreed. Somewhat placated, she allowed us to get her into her nightclothes and sleeping bag, asking us why the fox was considered bad. What had he done? It didn't take long for her to fall asleep. For a three-year-old who loved stories that anthropomorphise animals, it was hard to understand the importance of training to be a hunter in a hunting society.

Gusty cold winds predominated during our last week on Devon Island. I spent more time inside the tent with Pauline, teaching us string games such as 'Cats Cradle', a traditional way of providing entertainment in the igloo where space is tight. Using a loop of string held around her wrists, she manipulated it, opening and closing both hands

Tempy plays string games with Pauline.

to thread it between her fingers, producing an impressive fox, bear and dog. Other times, we went for walks on the tundra, finding fossils and huge petrified whale bones scattered on the raised beach. Once, Danny and Orla, on a walk, found the remains of eleven whales, 'I think they were mainly bowhead,' he said. 'Scattered around the area north of our camp. Almost certainly the result of ancient tidal strandings.'

While the Akeeagok family gathered lots of meat for the coming winter when it would be in short supply, I was content to do little other than reflect on our experience in this little-known part of the world. After all the hectic activity of preparing and then travelling throughout the spring and summer, it would soon be time to leave for our home in Ireland, but Danny wanted to stay for another year.

'It's such a great place; now that we are set up, we should take advantage of the opportunity to stay longer,' he said as we lay in the tent, looking out at Oisín contentedly chewing a raw caribou ear.

'We can't, our visas will expire soon.'

'But we'll never get this chance again,' he said.

'Who knows? I'm grateful we had the chance to live here for a year, but I couldn't face another winter now. Anyway, it's impossible, we have no money. We must return home.'

'You know, I was thinking we've reintroduced dog teams to Grise Fiord pretty much like Qitdlarssuaq reintroduced some old ways in Greenland,' Danny said, picking up a stone to examine the scallop shell fossil imprinted on it. 'So many people in Grise have been admiring the way our dog team is our only mode of transport.'

'Oh, I don't know if I'd go that far.'

'Well, Larry has a team, but he doesn't have time to use them, and I think the two new owners will use their teams to go hunting, for bears anyway.'

When we got back to Grise Fiord, our last week was spent packing, offloading things we couldn't take, and visiting friends. Unless you had a boat, it wasn't possible to go out hunting and more people were confined to home. I called to visit Mimi Akeeagok, who told me she was going to hunt narwhal. I was curious about the system for regulating the hunting of these small whales.

'My name was picked out from a hat. The Hunters and Trappers had two tags, and my name was pulled out.' She bounced baby April on her knee while we sat on the sofa. 'Tomorrow is my day!'

'Has anyone seen any whales?'

'Nah, I don't think so. I have three days with that tag to catch a *narwhal*,' she said. 'And my sister Syla got the other tag.'

The next morning, I saw her running out of the school where she teaches to the boat that Seeglok, her husband, was loading up with guns and fuel. A pod of *narwhal* had been located close by and she wasted no time in getting into the boat, starting the outboard motor and off they went. She returned later in the day, towing the dead *narwhal*, a beautiful, spotty, mottled creature, about four metres in length, with a long, spiral, spear-like tusk, which is actually an elongated tooth, coming from its upper jaw. A crowd gathered on the beach with knives, and the whale was skinned. Thick slabs of the skin, or *maktaaq*, were cut into smaller cubes and passed around so everybody got to taste the catch.

As I walked back from the Co-op the following day, with the sun low in the sky, I met a group of women gathered outside Ooleesie's house chatting and laughing in the golden afternoon sunshine, Annie called me over, inviting me to take part in their 'maktaaq' feast. A chunk of rubbery skin lined with a layer of juicy pink blubber lay on cardboard; Ooleesie cut it into small bite-sized pieces with her *ulu* and everyone tucked into this highly rated delicacy. I selected the smallest piece and chewed it; the flavour was subtle and nutty, but unable to break down the rubbery lump, I swallowed it whole. Annie cut some pieces into smaller slivers, for Orla and Oisín, who loved it.

Annie feeds Orla maktaaq, watched by Meeka and baby Lisa.

Again, sometime later, when Syla's *narwhal* was caught, we went down to the beach to join the people gathered there and they invited me to have a share. I took the smallest slab of *maktaaq* I could find, planning to boil it. Meeka fed some pieces to Orla and I asked her what usually happens to the rest of the whale meat.

'We don't eat that much,' she said. 'Just sometimes, if it's dried. We usually give it to the dogs. We don't like to waste any meat. We like giving it to other families if they don't have any, and we save the rest for winter, in the dark season, when we can hardly get anything.'

'I guess we're just like any other Inuit; it's just our culture,' Annie's daughter Lisa added.

'We're very grateful to you all for sharing with us,' I said. 'But I'm going to boil this to make it tender and easier to swallow.'

'Sure, that's good too,' Meeka laughed. 'Tastes like boiled eggs.'

The day before our departure, we visited our dogs. For Danny, they had been constant companions since the first day we arrived in the Arctic. He had put huge effort into their training and wellbeing, taking them out almost every day, and he knew each individual dog's character, traits, behaviours and temperament. The effort paid off; they safely took us on journeys of hundreds of kilometres across the ice, doing what they love – pulling sledges. Now with new owners, they were being well looked after and would have many more adventures out hunting.

On the last day of August, after our final farewells to our friends we boarded the weekly Twin Otter scheduled flight for the first leg of our long journey home. Irish Dresden, a company that produces fine porcelain figurines in County Limerick, generously came to our rescue by paying our return airfares. Danny, in return, would make two limited-edition sculptures for the factory. Although excited at the thought of seeing my family again, I would nonetheless miss Grise Fiord, the entire community, their sense of togetherness, their harmony with the environment and the animals they hunt, and the elders, full of life experience and traditional knowledge, who guide the next generation. They certainly prioritise the things that matter most in life. I had no idea what to expect when I arrived here; I didn't imagine I would gain a whole new insight into a unique vision of life. And, I had never felt so alive while journeying through that vast, challenging, stark landscape, not knowing what was ahead of us. In our western lives, we rarely get the chance to explore the unknown, and our growing disconnection from nature and especially from each other is a major cause of unhappiness. A sudden wave of reluctance to rejoin the big, wide world surprised me. But I wondered if this way of life could survive in our materialistic, globalised planet, and even more so today, in a place being transformed by climate breakdown.

I still had a lot to learn about life here, but I had an inkling that our year in Grise Fiord wouldn't be the end of our Arctic exposure.

Leaving Grise Fiord.

Epilogue

On our way home to Ireland, we camped for a few days near the beach in Resolute Bay, behind the half-finished South Camp Inn, awaiting our flight to Iqaluit, and from there, Montreal, London, Dublin, and eventually home in West Cork. This long journey allowed us to transition to settled life again and refamiliarise ourselves with routines, boundaries and expected behaviours from children. I had a hint of this when we stayed with a friend in Iqaluit, awaiting the next stage of the journey. Orla ran up in delight to his large goldfish swimming in a small tank, 'can I eat it?' she asked, nose pressed to the glass. 'She's like an Inuk,' he laughed. Later, when we queued at a long check-in line at Heathrow Airport, the children, tired after the long transatlantic flight, lay down on the floor, or on our bags and slept just as Inuit children do when they are sleepy, but this was met with tut-tutting from those behind in the line-up.

Back at home, in the rugged, treeless hills of the Beara Peninsula, facing the open Atlantic, we imagined it in a colder climate where the sea in front of our house would freeze, and we would hitch up our dogs and form a straight line across to the Sheeps Head Peninsula, then on to the Mizen for a picnic before rushing back home again. But work awaited us. Danny made models of two figurines of Orla and Oisín in their traditional Arctic clothes for Irish Dresden in Limerick as repayment for our return airfares, and I went to work as a locum GP in the West Cork area. Tempy went back to school in Cahermore with her old friends, and everyone settled into life in Beara. But Danny always planned on returning to Grise Fiord to paint, and eight years later, he brought Orla and Oisín with him to spend two months there in April/May – the most beautiful time in the Arctic. They stayed with Jaypetee and Anne, the children even going to school there and went out hunting on the sea ice by skidoo whenever the opportunity arose.

In 1999, Danny returned with Oisín, who was now ten years old. They celebrated the creation of the new Territory of Nunavut and went on exciting hunting trips, returning with dramatic photographs of beluga whales trapped in a small polynya, an opening in the sea ice on Jones Sound. Unable to swim beneath the ice as far as the distant open water, they struggled to find space to come up for air, Danny told me, and if that wasn't enough to distress them, several polar bears came to hunt. Some were dragged out by the bears, others sustained injuries, especially deep claw marks on their skin. It was reckoned there were up to fifty whales trapped, a sad sight. Seeglok, other Inuit, and Danny tried to help by widening the polynia, there was not much else they could do until the ice melted weeks later, allowing the surviving whales to escape.

Meanwhile, I worked part-time as a locum GP, but as the children grew older, I needed full-time work. I got a job in Community Health for the West Cork area which involved a long commute every day as well as getting trains up to Dublin to study part-time for a Master of Public Health degree (MPH). When I finished the MPH, I began to feel restless. The long daily drives were unsustainable, and I needed a new plan. Then Danny showed me a job advertised in a Nunavut newspaper for an Assistant Chief Medical Officer of Health for the Government of Nunavut. It looked interesting, had better pay, too, and I could walk to work. I sent in my application.

'Why are you applying for this job? I'm not moving to Canada.' Tempy protested as I drove her to school in the morning on the way to work.

'Don't worry, I won't get it.' I said, confident that I would not hear back from Nunavut.

But I was offered the job, and Tempy was adamant that she would stay in Ireland. Once again, our timing for going away was terrible for her; she was entering her final year at the local Scoil Phobail Bheara and had set her sights on attending the National College of Art and Design in Dublin afterwards. Orla and Oisín had not long started post-primary school, and they were interested in moving to Canada. Once again, we had a predicament. My intention was to be away for one or two years, with a leave of absence from my job in West Cork.

We reached a compromise, Tempy would stay with my mother in Newbridge and sit her Leaving Certificate exam there. Meanwhile, she would join us in Iqaluit for Christmas and the summer holidays. She did visit us, but hated the long journey; she was distancing herself from us with her own plans for the future, and we accepted that. We returned to Beara after two years to be nearer Tempy and to spend time with my sister, who had been diagnosed with a metastatic cancer. I found work in the Department of Public Health in Cork City, but after a few months, Orla, now sixteen, couldn't settle in school in Beara; she wanted to go back to Inuksuk High School in Iqaluit. Realising that nothing was happening regarding moving back, she arranged to go there herself and stay with her best friend in Iqaluit. Now, I found myself living in Cork City, away from Danny and Oisín in Beara for five days a week, not seeing Tempy, who had settled in Dublin as a student, and barely having time to see my sister in Kildare, while Orla was living far away in Iqaluit. This was not what any of us wanted. I got my old job back in Iqaluit, as it had only been temporarily filled for a year, and we were off again to live there for the next ten years.

Orla and Oisín finished high school there, Danny painted, going on long trips out on the sea ice on his skidoo, and I worked in the Department of Health, a challenging yet rewarding job that deepened my understanding of the problems faced by the indigenous population adjusting to being part of a bigger capitalist society with different goals and values. But the Inuit have always been resourceful and adaptable, and having their own self-government goes a long way towards resolving these problems. The community of Grise Fiord continues to thrive. Some of our friends, the elders, have died, but whenever we get the chance to go to Iqaluit, we meet people from Grise Fiord – the cost of getting to that community today is prohibitively expensive. All are proud of that little blonde five-year-old boy, PJ Akeeagok, Anne and Jaypetee's son, who is now the premier of Nunavut.

Looking back on my time living in Grise Fiord, I realise that much of my energy, at least in the early days, was spent resolving complications and setbacks, big and small, which are part of life for everyone. Danny had ambitious plans, but I was worried about exposing the children to hardship. At the same time, we both understood each other's perspective, we had to compromise and work together to move forward, just as Inuit do to survive in this tough environment.

And as Navarana pointed out, opportunities to test our abilities are essential. How can you know what you are capable of if you don't try?

Bibliography

AUDLALUK, Larry, *What I Remember, What I Know*. Inhabit Media Inc. 2020

BRUEMMER, Fred, *The Long Hunt*. The Ryerson Press Toronto. 1969.

CARPENTER, Edmund, *Eskimo Realities*. Holt, Rinehart and Wilton. NewYork. 1973.

EBER, Dorothy, *Pitseolak: Pictures out of my life*. University of Washington Press, Seattle, 1972.

FAIRLEY, T. C., *Sverdrup's Arctic Adventures*. Longmans, Green & Co. London. 1959.

HARPER, Kenn, *In Those Days: collected writings on Arctic History*. Inhabit Media, Iqaluit/Toronto. 2013.

HERBERT, Marie, *The Snow People*. Barrie & Jenkins. London. 1973.

MALAURIE, Jean, *The Last Kings of Thule*. Jonathan Cape, London. 1982.

MARY-ROUSSELIÈRE, Guy, *Qitdlarssuaq; l'histoire d'une migration polaire*. Les Presses de l'Universitè de Montrèal. 1980.

MacRURY, Ian Kenneth, *The Inuit Dog: its provenance, environment, and history*. Scott Polar Research Institute, University of Cambridge. 1991.

McCLINTOCK, Leopold, *The voyage of the 'Fox' in Arctic Seas*. John Murray, London, 1908.

SANDIFORD GRYGIER, Pat, *A Long Way from Home; The tuberculosis Epidemic among the Inuit*. McGill-Queen's University Press, Montreal and Kingston. 1994.

SCHLEDERMANN, Peter, *Voices in Stone; A personal journey into the Arctic past*. The Arctic Institute of North America of The University of Calgary. 1996.

SERREZE, Mark C. *Brave New Arctic; The untold story of the melting North*. Princeton University Press. 2018.

SIMPSON, Myrtle, *Due North*. Victor Gollancz Ltd. London. 1970.

TESTER, Frank James, KULCHYSKI, Peter, *Tammarniit (Mistakes): Inuit Relocation in the Eastern Arctic 1930–63*. UBC Press. 1994.

GLOSSARY

Aglu = a seal breathing hole in the ice
Aiviq = walrus
Amauti = garment with a pouch for carrying babies
Angakkuq = Shaman
Aqsarniit = Aurora borealis
Atii = Let's go!
Auger = a tool resembling a large corkscrew for boring holes.
ATV = small all-terrain vehicle
Floe edge = area where sea ice meets open sea water
Ice-foot = wall or shelf of sea ice frozen to the shore
Iglu [igloo] = snow house
Igunaq = fermented seal or walrus meat
Inughuit = indigenous people of Northwestern Greenland
Inuit = indigenous people of Northeastern Canada
Inuk = indigenous person of Northeastern Canada
Inuktitut = language spoken by Inuit of Northeastern Canada
Inuktun = language spoken by Inughuit of Northwestern Greenland
Kakivak = three-pronged spear
Kamiik = sealskin boots
Kamiit = several sealskin boots
Kiviaq = fermented auk
Kanajuq = small fish or sculpin
Lead = a transient area of open water caused by a large fracture in the sea ice
Maktaaq = narwhal or beluga whale skin and blubber.
Mannguat = soft shoes that muffle the sound of footprints
Nanuk = polar bear
Naphtha = paraffin

Napook = crosspiece on sledge
Narwhal = small whales
Pack ice = ice mass floating on the sea, formed by smaller pieces freezing together
Pituk = rope on sledge that all the traces are attached to
Polynya = area of open sea water all year round
Qallunaat = non-Inuit people
Qallunaaq = non-Inuit person
Qamutiik = sledge
Qamutiit = sledges
Runners = part of the sledge that provides contact with the ground
Siniktuq = he/she is sleeping
Skidoo = snowmobile
Tide crack = fracture between an immovable ice foot and movable tidal sea ice.
Traces = ropes attaching dogs to the sledge
Tuktu = caribou
Ujjuk = bearded seal
Ulu = cresent knife
Ummingmaq = muskoxen